HOW TO SELL YOU

In this Series

Other titles in preparation

SELL YOUR BUSINESS

A step-by-step guide to achieving a successful sale

Robert Ziman

How To Books

British Library cataloguing-in-publication data
A catalogue record for this book is available from the British Library.

© Copyright 1994 by Robert Ziman.

First published in 1994 by How To Books Ltd, Plymbridge House, Estover Road, Plymouth PL6 7PZ, United Kingdom. Tel: Plymouth (01752) 735251/695745. Fax: (01752) 695699. Telex: 45635.

Note: The material contained in this book is set out in good faith for general guidance and no liability can be accepted for loss or expense incurred as a result of relying in particular circumstances on statements made in the book. The laws and regulations are complex and liable to change, and readers should check the current position with the relevant authorities before making personal arrangements.

Typeset by PDQ Typesetting, Stoke-on-Trent
Printed and bound by The Cromwell Press Ltd, Broughton Gifford, Melksham, Wiltshire.

Contents

List of Illustrations

Preface

The world of small business is infinitely varied and interesting but surprisingly little has been written about how to go about selling a business. Regularly I receive phone calls which start, 'I have never sold a business before, so how do I go about it?' or, 'I want to sell my business and I need some help,' or, 'I am trying to sell my business, what else can I do?' I have written this book to answer these questions.

The act of selling something to which you have dedicated years of effort, worry and concentration can be traumatic and deeply upsetting. Your business has become an integral part of your life; into it you have breathed profit and success. You have been responsible for all the good decisions and all the mistakes.

The book is addressed to all those thousands of you who make up the small business community whose businesses depend directly on your individual efforts. It is designed to offer practical help as you face the moment when you have to decide on your future, and make painful and difficult decisions. It gives practical pointers as to how to go about valuing, marketing and selling your business. It does not concern itself with the technical work of solicitors and accountants. It does not disappear into difficult jargon. It offers straightforward and helpful advice with useful tips.

Each chapter takes you another step further into the process until at the end the business sale has been completed. Each chapter finishes up with three brief case histories, drama from an amalgam of typical situations. This is followed by some points for you to mull over, and an action flow chart.

For eleven years I have worked as a business transfer agent, deeply involved in the small business community. I have visited, valued and advised literally hundreds of small family businesses, partnerships and sole traders, and witnessed at first hand successful smooth sales and nursed through difficult ones. This experience has often helped me to foresee sticking points in a sale and take action against them. I have been able to observe at first hand good as well as bad practices.

Finally I would like to thank all those small business owners who have unwittingly over the years contributed to my own experience and knowledge. I have enjoyed endless cups of tea and coffee on strange business premises, from a charcoal burner's hut to a zoo cage. I have had discussions about repeat business with a funeral director and been shown in all seriousness a toothless, blind and deaf guard dog. I have seen poisonous tarantula spiders on the mantelpiece and pet pythons in the cellar.

Whatever your own business, I hope you will find this book of value, and that it will help you achieve your own objectives.

Robert Ziman

Introduction

Selling a business is competitive, just as selling anything else. Any product put up for sale has to be prepared, marketed and made attractive to buyers. It is up to you to prepare your article for sale in such a way that the purchaser will choose your product over another. For every product there is a limit to the way it can be presented. It will have a certain bulk, a weight, a density; it may or may not be transportable. Above all it has to be worth selling. If the price is forced down below cost level for the product then that item will not be produced and will disappear from the market.

These principles apply just as much to businesses, even if they are less apparent. For most the property and its physical situation cannot be moved. This is something immutable. However, it can be enhanced. With only a pot of paint much can be done to make your property more attractive in the eyes and heart of a purchaser. There may be negative points but usually you can present your business in a more positive light at very little extra cost. For example you can replace light bulbs, door mat, welcome signs and so on.

It is vital that you are never a party to misrepresentation because when your buyer finds out, there is no possible way of retrieving the situation. Selling a business is just as competitive as selling any other product. There are buyers and sellers and the two have to get together to make a deal.

In this book I have traced the essential steps required to prepare your business for sale, to find a serious purchaser and to complete the transaction. We will examine those elements to be considered before the sale, during viewings, negotiations and the legal process.

There is no 'one' way to sell a business. Clearly there are many routes by which the desired result will be achieved. However there is a common pattern, and there are many tips and actions to pave the way through what is usually a traumatic experience. All would wish to avoid a situation at handover when you are shouting from one corner of your small shop that your purchaser is 'an evil man' whilst the purchaser is shouting that you are 'a witch' from the opposite corner. All the while the stock valuers are counting the cans of baked beans, bread, boxes of aspirins and so on. The telephone is ringing and your spouse is trying to calm you down.

Such mayhem is totally unnecessary. The process of selling a business requires steady nerves, a sense of proportion and a determination to succeed. To dither around is exhausting, whereas a clear decisive well planned approach can bring about the desired result with the minimum of trouble.

For convenience and clarity all vendors are addressed directly as 'you' and purchasers are referred to in the singular masculine form. Businesses are bought and sold in the name of a single person, partnerships of two or more and limited companies. For tax reasons, particularly, the business may be owned by a sole trader, by a partnership or by a limited company with the day-to-day control exercised by others than the 'on paper' owner. This book is addressed to the controlling owners of businesses rather than the 'on paper' owners.

I have deliberately restricted the ground covered. I am addressing the owners of really small businesses, mostly in the retail sector, where men, women and other members of a family rely heavily on each other's opinions and work closely together. The considerations and procedures for selling larger more formal businesses are much the same and their owners will find this book very helpful — even though the final deal may be more complex and involve staged payments, service contracts, guarantees and so on.

Each country has it own system for the transfer of the ownership of property and therefore there will be some local variations in the tasks performed by solicitors, business transfer agents and accountants. In this book I have used the English system. However, all the personal ramifications — the valuation and the many anxieties associated with selling your business — will be equally applicable to all wherever you have your business.

TYPICAL BUSINESS SALES

Here are three quite typical small business scenarios which will be used to illustrate various actions. Sometimes they will be used to pose questions, at other times to show the consequences of certain actions. I hope that they will be useful to arouse discussion and bring home the choices and opportunities which exist.

Chris and Joan's leasehold fish and chip shop
Characters: Chris and Joan with daughter Elizabeth (aged 14) and

son Matthew (aged 16).

Chris and Joan bought a leasehold lock-up fish and chip shop with redundancy money two years ago at the top of the market because it looked a good buy with good profits. When they bought the business the lease had four years to run before renewal. They have to rely on the business totally to pay the mortgage and their living expenses.

They knew nothing about being self employed or fish and chips before purchase and were taught by the previous owner. They thought it would be a good business to pass on to the children in due course if jobs became difficult especially as Matthew was a bit slow at school work. Chris finds he prefers to watch videos and is growing to hate preparing fish and chips and late evening work. Joan has never relished the perpetual need to clean and to their chagrin the children do everything to avoid helping in the business.

To add to their concerns sales and profits have fallen steadily since taking over.

Mabel's village post office

The village post office has been in the family for thirty years; Mabel inherited it twenty years ago when her father died. She is now 68 and knows she lacks the energy she once had. The business just about pays for her needs and she has a little capital in a building society. She has never married and has a number of married nieces and nephews in the area of whom she is very fond. The property is freehold, free from mortgage, but in a poor state of repair. Mabel enjoys being a significant person in the village.

Brian and Jill's freehold kennels

Characters: Brian and Jill with daughter Sue (aged 5).

Brian and Jill bought the freehold kennels with two acres four years ago thinking it would be a dream place to bring up their daughter and solve their personal differences. Brian is a builder so there was space for his materials and Jill loved animals.

They disagree about most things. Brian is untidy and leaves around heaps of building materials, rubble and rusty tools. Jill on the other hand loves the property and likes the place to look nice. She is very conscious of the need to keep up appearances for dog owners when they come to leave and collect their animals. Jill struggles with most of the work on the property, whilst caring for Sue. Brian tends to leave their own building improvements half done and saunters off to the pub where he is the leader of the darts team.

They are both successful in making money but only a portion is recorded in the accounts. The bookkeeping is always a mess. Unless something is done their marriage will end in acrimony.

1
Deciding Whether to Sell

WHAT THIS CHAPTER WILL TELL YOU

Some of the reasons which might be making you think about selling
are identified and that which is saleable is identified.

UNDERSTANDING THE URGE TO SELL

Usually there is more than one simple reason for thinking about selling
your business and property. Seldom is it so straightforward. There is
often a complex web of feelings and thoughts which has to be
disentangled before deciding even to look at the possibility of selling.

Your need to sell may be impelled by outside events and pressures.
For example a rise in the cost of a loan may make a financial
institution demand repayment and the business is your only asset. Or
you may be having to divide your assets because of divorce. There
may be a bereavement and the executors (or other members of your
family) may be unable to continue the business for all sorts of valid
reasons. There may be new regulations imposed by the government or
by Brussels which require expensive new equipment which your
business is unable to finance.

Nevertheless in most cases you will have choices as to whether to
try to sell now or to make changes before selling or to continue as
before or to close down. You may even refuse to face up to the
problem and just hope it goes away (which it will not). Most reasons
for selling apply equally whether you are a sole trader, a partnership
or owner of the shares of a limited company.

Understanding your reasons and emotions
Which of these apply to you?

- Another business or trade appears to offer better prospects. It

appeals to you and your family. Will it satisfy more easily long
held aspirations?

- The rewards of your present business give you insufficient returns
  to sustain your desired lifestyle.

- You are so fed up with one aspect of the business that this is
  making you grumpy about the whole enterprise. For example you
  are reluctant to make an early morning start which is essential
  for a successful newsagent. You so hate the cleaning of the shop,
  whilst enjoying the contact with customers, that it makes you feel
  sour all the time.

- You have continual rows with your partner about the stocking
  and running of the business.

- The break up of your marriage results in the need to sell the
  business to divide its assets.

- You have divided loyalties between the needs of your children and
  the demands of your business. You feel that days are too short to
  give proper attention to both and thereby satisfying neither.

- There is an unacceptable strain on partners and family members
  working too closely together, so that natural personal animosity
  and differing ambitions loom too uncomfortably large.

- You feel bitter about the demands the business makes and you
  desperately want to pursue other hobbies and activities.

- There are fundamental disagreements over the direction for the
  development (or contraction) of the business.

- There is total disillusionment about the effort required to run a
  business. (In one extreme case a purchaser of a business placed it
  back on the market after only one day.)

- You are worried that the trade or business is going to be
  overtaken by changes in technology or increased competition.

- Even without a doctor's warning you are becoming aware of a
  need to retire. Your doctor has told you that you should heed the
  warning of a mild heart attack or high blood pressure. A mild

illness has caused you to worry that you will no longer be able to cope with the business as competently as you would wish.

● Marital difficulties or family rows have become focussed on the business, although this has really nothing to do with them. You think that by disposing of the business this will solve the situation and make home life more acceptable.

● You see possible financial problems and you are depressed. Or you have inherited a large sum of money and now want to relax in luxury free from business worries.

● The main source of customers is moving away, becoming redundant or the area is going to be bypassed.

● There is an alteration in the ethnic or social mix of the neighbourhood which makes you feel alien in your surroundings.

● The illness of a parent, long standing friend or close relative whom you are unable to visit or help is disturbing you.

● You have become aware that business costs are rising out of control and the business is failing. You become acutely aware that if some action is not taken very quickly, the outstanding borrowing will overtake the value of the business and lead to bankruptcy.

● You are just looking for a satisfactory change of business.

Why the reason for selling is important

For some it will be easy to identify the precise reasons for selling. For others it may be very difficult to be clear about the real motive. Whatever your reason, or mixture of reasons, it is essential to be utterly convinced that your business must be disposed of in one way or another. Your prospective purchaser will want reassurance that you are genuinely going to go through with the sale. He will avoid becoming embroiled in the purchase if he suspects that you are likely to change your mind and withdraw.

Most purchasers pay close attention to the reason(s) you give for selling and in order to answer the almost inevitable question you need to have prepared an acceptable reason based on the truth of the situation. For example you can say 'running a fish and chip shop is a horrible greasy occupation and you are glad to get shot of it' or you can say 'you would now like to have a café after having a profitable fish and chips business for five years.' Both say much the same but leave quite different impressions.

If your purchaser suspects that you are insincere in your desire to sell then a possible sale may turn sour for no readily identifiable reason. Time spent identifying, and being able to explain convincingly, the reason for selling can prove valuable from the outset. You may find yourself having to repeat the reasons many times because your purchaser cannot understand why you are disposing of such an apparently profitable business with so much obvious potential.

IDENTIFYING YOUR TRUE REASONS

Setting aside time
Have you considered scheduling a specific time to discuss the future of your business and your reasons for considering selling it? This could be a family discussion, a discussion between partners or a formal board meeting. By briefing each party beforehand they would have prior knowledge and time to prepare some positive ideas. The subject is usually so important and has so many ramifications for the future of each individual, that there is seldom much benefit in having an 'on the wing' exchange of views. Your partners need time to come to terms with their feelings; decisions taken hastily can so easily be misunderstood or misinterpreted.

Calling on outside professionals
Have you consulted outside professionals, such as your accountant, solicitor, business transfer agent or a close friend with appropriate experience? From them you can garner more information about the price which your business is likely to fetch, about the legal costs and other expenses associated with selling.

Writing down the reasons
Have you thought to ask each person involved to *write down* what he considers to be the future for the business and what reasons there are for selling? Although this approach sounds easy it can be the most difficult to carry through. You may not find it easy to explain your thoughts on paper but it is precisely through making the effort that the real reasons for selling will become apparent for all to see. Follow up discussions based on the written word are likely to be more to the point than poorly thought out reasons spoken by people who may not be very used to verbalising ideas clearly and concisely.

Why are you selling?	
	Circle
Have you identified your reason to sell?	Yes/No
Are you sure they are the right reasons?	Yes/No
Have you consulted with family and others?	Yes/No
Are there any alternatives?	Yes/No
If the answer is NO to any of the above questions then try again.	

Fig. 1. Reasons for selling: a checklist.

Being convinced of the true reasons

Very often it is only when faced with talking and explaining feelings about the business that the real reasons come out and you become convinced of the need to sell. You may agonise through many discussions before reaching a firm decision and the reasons for it. Be honest with yourself. Recognise your feelings and the true facts about your business.

You may reach the conclusion that there is no need to sell and that selling is not the solution to your problems. Other ways forward may emerge. These could include employing a manager, buying out your partner, radically changing the nature of the business, reducing staff or even closing down.

VALUING YOUR BUSINESS

There is only one way to look at the asking price and that is realistically in the market place for businesses as it exists, not as you might like it to exist. Your hopes and ideas for future improvements have no part in deciding the market price, however much you would like them to. Genuine potential may make a business more attractive but will not add materially to its value although it should make it easier to sell.

Appeal of the trade

Some trades have a greater appeal than others and this will affect the price achieved. A business which requires a depth of knowledge and training is relatively less expensive than a similarly profitable business which requires less knowledge and training. For example, a butcher's business will be less expensive than a post office/general store providing a similar net income.

Regrettably not every business or business property has a market value because there may be no-one willing to buy. For example, a retail business in an inner city area liable to riots or gang violence may have little or no value even though the business has a good history of high profitability. It is not true that *any* business can be sold if the price is right. The business may be desirable, but there may be no-one willing to pay anything for it. Therefore the first consideration is to see if there is anything which another person might want enough to buy.

Don't take as a starting point what you paid for the business, adding on the money you have spent on improvements. Nor is it helpful to consider only what you owe to a bank. Nevertheless it would be odd if you completely ignored the price paid for the business, improvements costs and outstanding loans. Naturally you will want to get something back for all your hard work in developing and running the business.

Licensed and franchised businesses

Some businesses operate under a licence or franchise agreement and may only be saleable under certain specified conditions. Look closely at the terms of any such agreements to ensure that you, the franchisee or licensee, have the right to sell the business. There are many variations but most agreements require at the least the approval of your purchaser by the franchisor or licensor.

Value of the business

The value of the business is the sum of a number of parts. These include:

- property
- fixtures, fittings and equipment
- goodwill.

Assessing the value of your property

All businesses need to operate from some form of base. It could be from a lock-up leasehold retail unit, a van, a domestic garage, a kitchen table, a freehold warehouse, a pitch in a street market and so on. Somewhere there has to be a base.

For many businesses there is no value attaching to the property. For example, a leasehold industrial unit on an estate where there are already many vacant units is not likely to have a market value. If your business is moved to another base the property may even have a negative value and you may have to dispose of it at a loss. For example your business may have outgrown your freehold workshop and after moving to larger leasehold premises you had not got round to selling the old workshop. You might have been quite content to wait until the market for freehold workshops had picked up, but because you have now chosen to sell the business as a whole the old freehold premises might have to be unloaded at almost any price.

On the other hand the location of your business premises may have a considerable market value, regardless of the business itself. For example, a purchaser may be willing to pay a large sum for a leasehold retail shop which may be trading at a loss if it is in the centre of a major city shopping area.

In addition to its location, the structure and physical condition of the property, the local supporting amenities, the suitability of the property to the business and the conditions of tenure, all affect the value.

It is reasonable to assume that there is a value in almost all freehold property but even this may not be true for a derelict industrial site. A property held under a lease, however, cannot be assumed to have a value, and guidance from an estate agent, business transfer agent or chartered surveyor will be required.

Advice about any property value can only be given after a site visit and an inspection of the terms of the lease, for which a charge may be made.

Assessing the value of fixtures, fittings and equipment

All businesses need some equipment. The requirements range from a simple money pouch to complex electronic tills, from giant removal vehicles to sack barrows, from typewriters to desk top publishing computers, from sweet scales to vehicle hoists, from dump baskets to gondola shelving, from servovers to walk-in freezers and so on. Many items have little or no value if removed to auction but have an inbuilt value because they are fitted and on site. Other items may have been unknowingly overtaken by more stringent regulations, and therefore have no value and are due to be replaced.

Values for some equipment are quite simple to assess by reading trade press advertisements and contacting suppliers of new or secondhand equipment. Value for other equipment may need to be researched. For example the wide range of tools held by a tool hire business might require a lot of work to establish their market value. The figures on the balance sheet for your fixtures, fittings and equipment usually bear little resemblance to their market value and therefore are an unreliable guide.

As a general rule if you own fixtures and fittings which meet current legal requirements and are in regular use then they will have a monetary value. The amount should be more than the cost of replacement items in similar condition from the secondhand market because they are *in situ* and currently working for you.

Assessing the goodwill value

It is this item which generally causes the most difficulty when people try to assess the value of a business.

- Goodwill represents the demand for that business over and above the physical assets of the business.

There are many ways of calculating and considering goodwill. There are books written expounding many theories, from denial that goodwill exists to detailed complex algebraic formulae which few people can follow. The exact amount paid for the goodwill is sometimes easier to see *after* the business is sold than before.

For example a freehold retail store may be sold for £100,000 (excluding stock). The property value may be assessed by comparison with other similar sized local properties at say £65,000. The fixtures and fittings may be assessed at say £8,000 making a total of £73,000. Nevertheless a buyer is prepared to pay £100,000 and the only value left not assessed is the goodwill. Therefore this has to be worth £27,000.

Goodwill may be worth more to one purchaser than another. For example a business similar to the one above may be standing on a site onto which a neighbouring business wishes to expand. The neighbour may be prepared to pay £150,000 in order to secure the site whereas to anybody else this perfectly viable business may be worth only £100,000. For the one buyer the goodwill is valued at £77,000 (purchase price of £150,000 less the property £65,000, less the fixtures and fittings £8,000) whilst to all the others the goodwill is valued at £27,000 (purchase price £100,000 less property £65,000 less the fixtures and fittings £8,000).

Negative goodwill

The goodwill can even be a negative value. To give two examples:

1. A freehold property with a business may be worth less than if the property were a private residence. The cost of the conversion may be greater than the value of the business.

2. A poorly performing business is run from leasehold premises. In order to dispose of the responsibility for the rent the owner may be willing to pay somebody to take over the business and lease rather than ask for a payment.

Regrettably in areas of very depressed economic activity neither of these situations are rare.

Coping with reality
The above is all very fascinating, but how can you assess the goodwill value of your own business?

Getting help
You can approach the problem by asking for the assistance of outside persons. Accountants will calculate the goodwill from a theoretical standpoint based mainly on the trading accounts. Business transfer agents will calculate a probable good will figure based on the market price. Each agent and each accountant will have a different method of valuing your business and the goodwill. They may come to widely differing values, or the same values by widely differing routes.

If your business appears similar to many others being advertised for sale then you can obtain a rough idea from studying the 'for sale' columns and relating your business to the description of others being advertised. However you must be totally honest with yourself about your business when making such comparisons.

Estimating goodwill value
In most cases the goodwill value is directly related to the profitability of the business, the nature of the trade, terms of the lease and the position of the unit. The goodwill in a business with falling demand and requiring specialist skills eg a wet fish shop, will be less than in a business which is satisfying a growing demand eg debt collection. The goodwill in a fashion business held on a short six year lease will be less than a newsagents held on a longer fifteen year lease (all other factors affecting the price being equal).

Using the net income basis
Goodwill is the most difficult aspect of valuing a business and can vary through a wide band. Unless there are exceptional circumstances, however, the goodwill value rarely exceeds five times the annual true NET income; and most frequently is between one and three times the annual true NET income for a normal family run small business.

- The true NET income is the total shown in the Trading and Profit and Loss Account after all the essential business expenses have been paid and before any financing charges or owners perks and wages are taken off.

The value of a business

Business value with freehold property
= Freehold property (tangible)
+ Fixtures and fittings (tangible)
+ Goodwill (intangible)

Business value with leasehold property
= Leasehold property (intangible)
+ Fixtures and fittings (tangible)
+ Goodwill (intangible)

The intangible amounts are adjusted to make the total value of the business equal to the market value.

Fig. 2. Business value.

As already stated, outside professionals are often at loggerheads and in the end a commonsense pragmatic approach may provide the sensible answer.

Taking a look at the value of your stock

In addition to property, fixtures and fittings and goodwill, most businesses also hold stocks. The stock might be office stationery (a service business), goods for sale (a retail shop), or raw material for processing (a restaurant) or goods in course of manufacture. In order to produce meaningful accounts your stock has been valued each year, so you will have a good idea of its value in normal trading conditions.

If you have given your accountant a rough estimate of the total stock value each year end then you will need to make a realistic assessment now so that the stock value is not grossly over- or understated to prospective purchasers. When stock has to be sold off by auction or through a stock clearance sale, the cost values are seldom reached. Indeed, sometimes only a fraction of the original cost is realised.

In a retail business the stock value is easy enough to measure by reference to purchase invoices and the unsold saleable goods. Stock valuation becomes more complex in manufacturing as the value of unsold items has to be determined at each stage of production but there are recognised and accepted methods of stock and work in progress valuation.

With few exceptions a business is priced and offered for sale *excluding stock* because stock is so variable and will fluctuate from day to day or even hour to hour.

The money generated from the sale of the stock can be a very significant sum in relation to the total sale or it can be quite small. For example, the stock held in a fish and chip shop may be only £500 whereas a hardware store generating a similar net income may hold stocks valued at £20,000. Therefore the cash value of the stock is important when you are looking at the likely total proceeds arising from the sale of your business.

Intellectual copyright such as royalties, licences, patents, trademarks, know how and so on are really another form of stock but are normally lumped together under the general heading of goodwill.

SUMMARY

In the first part of this chapter possible reasons for you wanting to sell your business were outlined. This was followed by an explanation as to how an asking price can be arrived at.

You may have found that after looking critically at the value of your business that you have nothing to offer which could persuade a purchaser to part with money. The costs of selling may be greater than any net proceeds. The proceeds may not cover outstanding loans and overdrafts. It may be a pleasant surprise.

Whatever the result of this initial investigation it is vital to reach a firm and clear decision as to whether to proceed with trying to sell or to take some other path.

The choices are limited to closing the business, continuing as before, giving the business new direction and impetus, or trying to find a purchaser. Delay, lethargy and depression should not be allowed to creep over you because after making the effort to look carefully at the future of your business it is tempting to sit back and rationalise that nothing can be done. This is unhealthy for you and everyone else concerned with the business.

Finally you need to take action as to your future. Your goals need to be set and pursued with the single minded vigour and determination required by a person in business.

CASE STUDIES

Chris get a shock

Before going to sleep one night Chris suddenly has a brilliant idea to solve the family problems. He will sell the business. Next morning he puts an ad in the local newspaper. He states a price which is the total of what he paid plus the cost of the new range, the new walk-in chiller, last year's extravagant building improvements plus an extra

10% for all the work he put in. Sales and profits are not mentioned.

Chris does not receive any response except for a remark from one of his regular customers who said, 'I never thought you would stick it as long as you have, but you must be mad to think anyone would be such a sucker to pay that amount!'

He asks to see his landlord and tells him that he wants to close the business and give up the lease. The landlord curtly reminds Chris that under the lease Chris remains responsible for paying the rent until the lease expires in four years' time. Chris argues furiously but the landlord is adamant and suggests that Chris checks with his solicitor.

Chris goes to see his solicitor who confirms the position. Chris accuses him of not telling him about these terms before the lease was signed. The solicitor reminds Chris that he tried for an hour to explain that the landlord has no obligation to cancel the lease on request, and that he can also call on Chris for the rent if a buyer of the business later defaults. Chris recalls now that he was so sure that the business was what he wanted that he did not bother to listen.

Following this shock Chris decides to struggle on and try to sell. He now realises that if he closes the business there is little hope of receiving anything but a tiny premium which might just cover the cost of selling. Then he would be in deep financial trouble.

Mabel vaguely plans to sell

At age 68 Mabel thinks she ought to do something about the business which she has loved all her life. She feels she ought to sell the post office and see more of her nephews, nieces and their children. She does not know how to go about it so she puts a handwritten notice in the window, 'Business for sale'. All the village elders spend hours talking it over with her and giving conflicting advice.

Mabel receives one enquiry. She does not know what to say about the price and phones her accountant. He does not know either, but in a confident manner gives her a figure based on the very low profits. This turns out to be well below the market price for the property if it were sold as a private residence.

Jill gives Brian a household ultimatum

For Brian and Jill it is the last straw when their daughter Sue gets the measles. Jill faces Brian with an ultimatum which is that either you clear out or tidy up and do your share round the kennels. Brian replies by saying that they will solve their problems by selling and moving to a more suitable place he has seen. It is a super property at the other end of the village with a large barn ideal for all the building materials and an old shed which he will convert for next to nothing into a cattery for Jill to look after.

After yet another row they decide to try and sell at a price which will allow them to buy the other place without giving their present property away. To cut short any further argument about price they have the idea of calling in a business transfer agent to advise them and give them a realistic view of the market for selling businesses such as theirs.

POINTS FOR DISCUSSION

1. In view of their personalities what steps could Chris and Joan, Mabel, Brian and Jill have taken to identify what they could do apart from trying to sell?

2. In what circumstances would you decide to keep your business rather than try to sell it?

3. What positive factors made you decide to buy your business? Are they still valid?

Thinking of selling

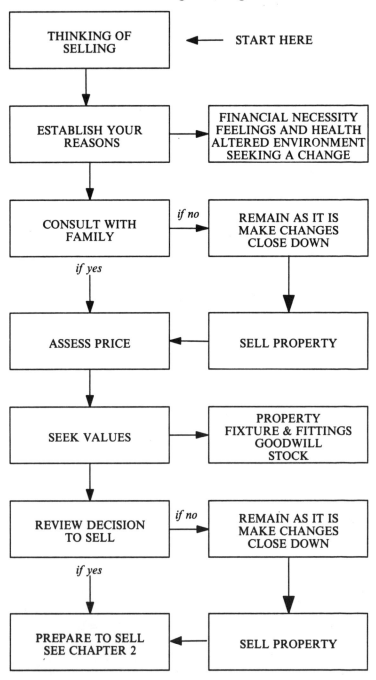

Fig. 3. Thinking of selling.

2
Preparing Your Business for Sale

WHAT THIS CHAPTER WILL TELL YOU

Selling a business, moving house, changing a lifestyle, and perhaps buying another business may take a week or as long as five years. Time and effort spent planning and preparing will prove of great value later because it will help clarify what has to be achieved. The first consideration is timing, followed by the gathering together of relevant documents and facts about your property, your business, and the market for selling businesses. All this will be looked at in this chapter, together with the costs of selling a business.

Preparation and planning are crucial if the aim of selling smoothly and with the minimum of anxiety is to be achieved.

DECIDING WHEN TO SELL

Seasonal factors
Many businesses by their very nature have peaks and troughs during the year. The pre-Christmas period and the immediate post-Christmas period obviously distort the monthly pattern of trading for most businesses. Sales figures, stock levels, staffing — all are affected up or down, and time may be so restricted that you will be unable to pay proper attention to prospective purchasers. Seasonal businesses are quiet or closed in the winter and very busy in the summer.

Other businesses may have January, Easter, Summer and Autumn sales. You will need time to meet potential purchasers and their advisers; time is required to prepare information for solicitors; time is required for you to decide what to do when the business is sold and so on. Business sales take place throughout the year although August, December and January are the quieter months.

Planning ahead

Your personal preferences will also affect the timetable for a business sale. Capital gains tax considerations, trading years, health, school year, school examinations, ages of the people concerned — all have a part to play in deciding when to place your business on the market.

In order to fix an ideal date by which to achieve a sale you need to plan well ahead. Six months to a year is quite normal from the date of placing a business on the market to agreeing a sale. Even after agreement you should allow three months for a sale with property involved to go through, particularly if loans are needed or references for a landlord. Even without the purchaser needing to sell a property there have been times when the sale of a business has taken as long as fifteen months. A survey may call for more detailed investigation of the property and quotations for repairs. The franchisor may be unable to arrange training for your purchaser. The sale may be subject to planning consents and so on.

Delays

Seemingly unavoidable delays arise even when both parties wish to hustle a deal through all its stages. A solicitor may go on holiday, illness strikes a referee and nobody is told, documents get lost during the local authority search, deeds cannot be released because proper notification has not been lodged and so on.

The list is long and varied, with at times some very bizarre excuses. For example the only key to a safe fell out of the pocket of a solicitor's daughter's swimwear when she was out playing and the safe manufacturer was on two weeks' shutdown.

Where there is no property involved (newsrounds, van sales and home based businesses) the selling process can be breathtakingly fast.

GETTING YOUR TRADING FIGURES READY

The most important relevant documents are the business accounts. You may have neglected these, regarding the keeping of your books as a chore to be done when time permits, and given them a low priority. However, when preparing a business for sale, keeping the accounts clear and up to date must have top priority. Few purchasers will even consider making an offer until they have seen trading figures and up-to-date evidence of sales. Purchasers tend (often with some justification) to be suspicious of trading figures given verbally or on the backs of brown paper envelopes.

Recorded sales

Sales which are not reflected in the accounts have no place in the asking price for a business when it is offered for sale. It is useless telling a purchaser that the business is taking £4,000 per week when the accounts show only £2,500 per week. It is important to keep your account book totals up-to-date. Daily takings, weekly, monthly or quarterly totals for your current trading year need to be available for viewing by an interested prospective buyer.

- Copies of the most recent VAT returns are good acceptable evidence of sales during the current financial year or where there is an absence of trading accounts.

Briefing your accountant

As soon as your financial year ends you need to pass all the documents and accounting records quickly to your accountant and have the **trading and profit and loss account** prepared and available for your agent and any prospective buyer. Tell your accountant that you are considering selling and ask him to prepare the accounts quickly, at least in draft form. Most accountants will appreciate the reason for such a request and try to give the accounts priority over other work. Should your accountant appear slow, then exert pressure to make sure you have what you need. Many sales are lost because accounts which should have been available cannot be produced.

You may be tempted to delay your annual accounts until the business is sold and have a single set of accounts prepared covering your final fifteen to eighteen month trading period. This could prove to be a false economy. Your purchaser may need to have the accounts to satisfy his lending source, his advisers or his bank, and you may then find yourself paying your accountant an extra fee. Unless a sale is imminent it is best to maintain the normal pattern for preparing your annual accounts.

The availability of sales figures, profit graphs and photocopies of the relevant documents can make a favourable impression on a purchaser when he visits your business for the first time. A good impression may well be marred if you are unable to lay your hands on a copy of the accounts. Searching through a grubby pile of envelopes for accounts referring to two years ago leaves a purchaser with a terrible impression of inefficiency and muddle, not a good start for a possible sale. In the preparation stages, therefore, you may have to change long established habits and ensure that up-to-date and accurate trading figures are kept.

Looking at the purchaser's need for accurate figures

Why is so much emphasis and importance placed on the historical trading record of the business when selling? To you the potential of the business is obvious, so why bother with the trading accounts referring to activity which is all in the past? The reason is that past performance of the business is the only factual guide to the money-making capability of your business which is acceptable to the purchaser, his financial advisers and his bankers. There are other reasons as well.

- The saleability of a business depends on its appeal and its price. The price must relate to the **financial returns** and the buyer has to know the trading figures in detail to decide if this relationship is acceptable and the business likely to be viable.

- A purchaser usually wants **proof** that the business is really trading to the level he has been told. Most purchasers are cautioned not to accept sales figures by word of mouth and are reassured by seeing professionally prepared accounts. The stories of people who have bought businesses without taking these elementary precautions are so legion that most buyers have become suspicious about any discrepancy between what they are told and what is in the accounts.

- Most business buyers need to raise **loans**. Almost without exception banks and finance houses want copies of accounts prepared by an accountant. When a business has been closed and the property still has a value, or when a business has only been trading for a very short period, the lending source will seek the reassurance of an independent specialist valuation (paid for by the prospective purchaser).

- It is difficult for a prospective purchaser to make a business plan and budget without the guidance of historical accounting figures; the only people who can provide the information are you and your accountant.

- Many purchasers will not even consider making an offer for a business until they have discussed the accounts with their own accountant or financial adviser; many are totally guided by their advice. This advice cannot be given without the accounts.

It is important therefore to overcome any feelings of reluctance and it is reasonable for you to ask the prospective purchaser not to hand round the accounts to all and sundry. Should you give a prospective purchaser your accounts to take away you will find that they are rarely returned in spite of promises to the contrary. Consequently never give anyone your original signed accounts and only provide photocopies. Most accountants will charge heavily if asked for additional copies.

Revealing income not recorded in the accounts

You may be concerned about passing such confidential information to prospective purchasers because you feel it is private and you should not like it to become common knowledge. Undeclared sales have no place in accounts and thus no place in the sale of your business. Telling a viewer how much you are taking which is not in the accounts only serves to tell the viewer that you are a cheat and out for what you can get. It does little to help the sale because the purchaser has to be convinced by evidence.

Two sets of 'accounts'
Some business owners even go so far as to maintain two sets of accounts, one set for the tax computation and one set for their own gratification. Should you feel the need to discuss such matters with a viewer you will need to be very cautious. The prospective purchaser could be a tax inspector or even a thief seeking out a business hiding a large sum of poorly protected undeclared cash.

SELLING A FRANCHISE

Franchises cover a very wide and growing range of businesses and the terms of every franchise are specific to that franchise. Most franchises give you the right to sell the franchise; some however include a clause stating that you must offer the business to the franchisor first, and can only offer the franchise on the market with his permission.

The franchise agreement usually sets conditions which have to be satisfied before a purchaser is accepted. The terms may specify training requirements, payment of training fees, changes in area, changes in method of operation and so on. You will need to remind yourself of the detail so that you will be able to explain it clearly and with confidence to any potential purchaser. Bumbling around and being very unsure will fail to impress anyone and make you feel uncomfortable.

Sub Post Offices

Some businesses are not formal franchises, but the selling process is similar to a franchise. The most obvious examples are sub post offices where the sale will depend on the new owner being approved by the Post Office. A not dissimilar case is a newsround where the new owner has to be accepted as a customer by the sole supplier of newspapers for the area.

Saving time
Your purchaser may insist on obtaining the approval of the franchisor before initiating the legal conveyance for any property involved. This can greatly lengthen the time your sale takes to go through. If a high level of trust can be generated between you and your purchaser there is normally no reason why the franchise approval process and the property/business conveyance cannot run concurrently.

PREPARING THE ASSETS FOR SALE

The property
Your property must be looked at with a critical eye. Remember, your purchaser will be seeing it for the first time and you want him to carry away a good impression. If the first impression of the outside and inside is pleasing, this feeling will stay with the viewer and influence his judgment in your favour through any subsequent negotiations.

If the first impression is unfavourable then logic and argument have to be stronger during any negotiations which follow. There are always small improvements which require only a little extra effort.

- For example, clean windows, tidy stockroom shelves, the disposal of loose packing materials, the removal of old tatty posters, fresh paint over that old eyesore, garden lawn cut and so on.

- Any clearly visible and more expensive repairs to the property should be completed before it is offered for sale. For example any rotten or unpainted barge boards and window frames should be attended to, damaged concrete and wooden steps replaced, old kitchen and bathroom tiling renewed and generally the property should be presented in a reasonably acceptable decorative order.

This catalogue of items may appear to be a heavy burden but any improvement which can be made before placing the property on the market may prove to be worth the effort. Purchasers are not impressed by seeing a half decorated room (which you promise to finish), a stockroom stuffed with old and rotting cardboard to be cleared out. They are much more impressed by seeing the room fully decorated and pleasantly furnished, the stockroom all neat, the rear yard free of broken down freezer cabinets.

It may be tempting to promise a prospective purchaser during the viewing that the building work will be finished before the sale is completed, that those rusty old vans will be removed. How much better it is if the renovation work has been completed and the junk disposed of before the puchaser comes to view.

For most purchasers the prime anxiety is about the business's viability and potential. They may be willing to take on a less than perfect building but will still sigh with relief if the property, which in many cases will become their home, appears in good order. They can then move in without the need for costly repairs and new decorations upheaval as they take on a new venture.

Weighing up the cost of improvements
Money spent on sealed double glazed windows or an expensive new shop front is unlikely to be recouped by upping the market price of the business. Such expensive improvements are more likely to make your business saleable than to raise the achieved price significantly.

The purpose of most property improvements should be for you to enjoy the benefit, not to make a profit. There is a parallel with buying a new car. As soon as you have driven a new vehicle off the garage forecourt the value of the car falls but you benefit from its use, its greater comfort, its increased reliability and so on. Similarly there is depreciation when new shop freezers, new tills, new shop front are installed.

Where the business or accommodation is in very poor condition or is in really genuinely superb condition the selling price will markedly reflect these extremes. For example, a shop with old bent and twisted painted wood shelving and irregular wood floor would fetch far less than a comparably profitable shop with a smooth carpeted floor, modern metal shelving and concealed lighting. Even in this example the difference in selling price between the shops is likely to be *less* than the cost of a refit of the former. However the latter is likely to sell more readily than the former.

Therefore any work which is put in hand with the specific purpose of easing a sale needs to be carefully costed. It needs to be recognised that the costs for the improvements are unlikely to be recouped by blindly adding them in full to the marketing price which was set prior to the improvements. Some of the costs may be recovered by giving you a better bargaining position but the real benefit of the improvements should show up with an easier sale. The small cosmetic improvements about the property are going to make the greatest impression.

Arranging your own survey
It is debatable whether it is worth going to the trouble or expense of having a **structural survey** on the property before placing the business on the market to find out in detail about its condition. With this knowledge it becomes incumbent upon you to answer the purchaser's questions about the property accurately; any deliberate misinformation could lay you open to a criminal prosecution. It is also true that if you have your own survey you will be in a stronger position to counter any points raised by the purchaser and to resist pressure for a price reduction.

Neither a serious purchaser not his lending source are likely to accept your survey.

The business unit
Much of the above will apply equally to an industrial unit. A neat, clean and well presented business will always appeal to a purchaser more than a dirty, untidy and messy unit.

Food preparation areas
Do exercise particular care in any premises where food preparation takes place. A freezer whose door will not shut properly because of a build up of ice is a poor advertisement for the quality of the food sold. If you are seen to be flagrantly ignoring basic food handling hygiene the prospective buyer will be put off. But if the food preparation areas are spotless, food handling course certificates displayed, all food neatly stored in proper containers, cleaning materials put away and so on, then you will promote confidence in the soundness of the enterprise.

Flooring
Attention should be paid particularly to the flooring. A poor, rough or sticky floor leaves a bad impression with the purchaser failing to recognise the precise source of his discontent. New floors and floor coverings can be expensive and very disruptive to install, but the effort and cost may well prove of benefit in terms of finding a purchaser more quickly who is willing to offer a good price. Even if the business takes longer to sell than anticipated you will benefit in the meantime from easier to maintain premises and in all probability from increased sales.

Checking the property

Have you looked to see what can be done to improve

	Circle
The walls	Yes/No
The ceiling	Yes/No
The floor	Yes/No
The entrance	Yes/No
The windows	Yes/No
The lighting	Yes/No
The heating	Yes/No

Fig. 4. Preparing the property for sale.

Fixtures, fittings and equipment

The same good housekeeping principles apply. Clear out those old bits of shelf fittings and ancient cash register from the shed. Only retain those accumulated spare fixtures and items which are in a presentable condition and could genuinely be useful. Using the argument that there is a faint chance that the tatty old freezer cabinet (which has broken down) might one day be useful is just an excuse for indolence. Your purchaser will not thank you for leaving it to him to get rid of your junk. Since the problem will not go away it is better to tackle it sooner rather than later.

In your own mind, sort each item of the fixtures, fittings and equipment into one of three categories. Do the same with the domestic furnishings when living accommodation is included as part of the sale:

- Those items which are definitely included and are essential for the daily operation of the business, eg shelving, dairy deck, label pricing guns, till, built-in-cooker.

- Those items which are definitely not included, eg microwave, chest freezer, curtains, pictures, washing machine. To illustrate this more clearly: if you own a pub or restaurant you may have hung some of your own pictures in the public areas to give the bar a more personal atmosphere. If so, decide which pictures are to be included and which you will keep. Family agreement must be secured at the outset, because later if there is seen to be dissent within your family your purchaser will become dismayed and possibly withdraw.

- Those items which may be available for sale by separate negotiation, eg van, domestic curtains, floor coverings. These are items which you may be pleased to renew if the price is right or be prepared to use as bait during the selling negotiation to raise a low offer up to an acceptable level.

Checking the fixtures, fittings and equipment	
	Circle
Have you got rid of all the junk items?	Yes/No
Does all your equipment satisfy the regulations?	Yes/No
Is every item as clean and presentable as possible?	Yes/No
Have you listed what items are to be included?	Yes/No
Have you listed what items are negotiable?	Yes/No
Have you listed what items are not to be included?	Yes/No
Do all your family agree with the listings?	Yes/No
Have you checked the leasing/finance agreements?	Yes/No

Fig. 5. Preparing fixtures, fittings and equipment for sale.

OUTSTANDING LEASING/FINANCE AGREEMENTS

Where equipment is being purchased on a lease/purchase agreement, you may decide to pay off the balance out of the proceeds of the sale. When there is a significant sum to be paid, settling the debt or transferring the agreement to the purchaser can become part of the overall negotiation. However, remember to check the terms of your agreement with the loan company because some agreements do not permit a transfer or else attract a charge.

Some agreements entered into are for leasing only and may or may not permit the transfer of the lease to another party.

Maintenance agreements

Agreements covering security alarm systems, security cameras and monitors may be a combination of maintenance with lease/purchase or maintenance with part rental and part owned or just maintenance. As soon as you have a moment, familiarise yourself with the exact terms of any agreement and guarantees. Only then can you speak confidently and correctly, and give your purchaser accurate information.

Checking all the documents	
	Circle
Have you copies of your last three years accounts?	Yes/No
Have you a copy of your lease?	Yes/No
Have you a copy of all finance/lease agreements?	Yes/No
Have you a copy of your franchise agreement?	Yes/No
Have you copies of any machine guarantees?	Yes/No
Have you copies of any property repair guarantees?	Yes/No
Have you copies of any Local Authority permissions?	Yes/No
Have you copies of up to date sales graphs?	Yes/No
Have you copies of up to date sales figures?	Yes/No

Fig. 6. Documents which may be needed.

Gathering together the relevant documents

If the original agreements and guarantees cannot be found then apply for copies.

The solicitors preparing the contract of sale will require all the documentation concerning any financing or leasing arrangements, guarantees and all other agreements which are being transferred.

Outdated equipment on lease/finance

Often equipment is outdated and fails to perform to a standard required by law. If you have any doubts consult your local trading standards officer or environmental health officer. You should replace or have repaired all inadequate equipment (for example a freezer which fails to maintain the correct temperature) rather than be forced to face up to it later. Making false or misleading statements is dangerous and illegal. Therefore any written or verbal comments about the equipment have to be factual and accurate. It will be extremely unpleasant to receive a vigorous communication from a solicitor about misleading the purchaser once you thought the business and all its associated problems were well behind you.

HOW TO SELL A LIMITED COMPANY

Many small businesses have been formed into private limited companies with the ownership of the shares held by members of a family. If this is your situation you have to choose between

- offering for sale the business *with the limited company* or

- offering the business only *whilst retaining the limited company.*

The latter choice means that the business is sold *by the limited company.* You may later decide to wind up the company, or to retain and use it for another business. Alternatively the business being sold may be one part of a larger concern which is being retained by the limited company. An example is when the business being sold is one retail unit out of a chain of retail units owned by the limited company. When such a business entity is sold and the limited company is retained then the involvement of solicitors and accountants is similar to a sale by a sole trader or partnership.

Selling your shares

The former choice means that you will in effect be selling *your shares in the limited company* and thus the ownership passes with the shares to your purchaser. This is more complex and the costs of selling may prove greater. On the other hand, selling your shares in the company may prove to be more tax efficient. Hence the need to consult your accountant before any irrevocable action is taken.

The precise value of your shares involves drawing up a balance sheet on the day of handover. This means that the purchaser pays you a sum for your shares in the business, adjusted to take into account all debtors and creditors. If there is property your purchaser will no doubt require a survey and request solicitors to make local authority and title searches in the usual way.

- You will be asked to sign a complex statement agreeing the truth of the accounts and giving safeguards to your purchaser against undeclared shortcomings.

- You will be asked to confirm that the limited company has fulfilled all its legal requirements in respect of taxes and returns.

- You may even be asked to accept an interim payment for the business until the final balance sheet has been prepared and agreed by the accountants.

ESTIMATING THE COSTS OF SALE

Taxation and selling costs can vary according to how you sell your business. To avoid disappointment later do seek the advice of your accountant — even before placing the business on the market. After all, what concerns you most is the final total, after costs, you are likely to receive from the sale. The cost of making the sale could well influence your decision when it comes to accepting or refusing an offer.

How VAT affects the costs of selling

Most quotations for costs will state a fixed sum or a percentage of the selling price. Check whether the figure quoted includes or excludes VAT. If you are registered for VAT then the VAT can be reclaimed from the Customs & Excise. However if your turnover is such that you are not registered then the VAT element on any selling cost has to be considered. For example a hair salon with a turnover of £33,000 per year can be quite profitable and still not be VAT registered. Since the owner is not able to reclaim the VAT element on the solicitor's and the agent's fees his selling costs will be higher than for another business sold for a similar price which is registered for VAT.

Dealing with leasing/finance agreements

In many loan and mortgage agreements, charges are imposed when the loan is repaid early. The terms for any such charges should have been clearly stated in your agreement or mortgage deed. If in any doubt contact the lender and get the position clarified. Conjecture can lead to expensive mistakes.

Assessing your tax liability

Your accountant needs to be consulted about any tax liability which could arise from the sale. In particular you must be aware of any liability for **capital gains tax** based on the increased value of the business during your period of ownership and how any such liability can be mitigated (reduced).

Sale of living accommodation
No capital gains tax is payable on any living accommodation which is sold provided it is your principal dwelling. The division of the selling price between the business and your private property must be realistic because all sales are later scrutinised by the **District Valuer** to ensure that the amount of the total sale ascribed to the living accommodation is comparable with similar living accommodation in the area. If the valuer considers that the amount ascribed is loaded to avoid a CGT liability for the business then you will, *up to five years after the sale*, receive a demand for the tax. This could run into several thousand pounds. You will then have to go to the expense of fighting

the District Valuer to convince him that the apportionment of the selling price was reasonable in relation to property prices at that time.

Assessing any capital gains tax liability

Capital gains tax liability is reduced on account of age or illness and there are strict rules for **rolling over** (deferring) the gain into another business. The detail of all such regulations changes most years with the Chancellor's Budget. It is difficult to be conversant with all the small print without the help of an accountant.

Costing the services of your accountant

Whenever the expertise of others is needed you can reasonably ask for a quotation (or at least an indication) of the likely charges. This can be in writing although some accountants are only willing to state the formula by which they calculate their charges. If you are unaware of this you could have quite a shock at the final total, and question how such a large fee can be justified. When a fixed quotation has not been provided, insist on being kept fully informed of the charges as they mount up.

Changing accountants in the middle of a sale, or negotiation with the tax authorities, can be unwise as it could arouse suspicions that you have something to hide. Staying with one accountant, however expensive, may prove cheaper in the long term and the better option because he is familiar with all the background of your business. A new accountant has to spend time sorting this out. Nevertheless if you are thoroughly dissatisfied with your accountant and have lost all confidence in him then you must consider a change.

Costing the services of your solicitor

Solicitors are usually prepared to give a reasonably firm quotation for the work of conveyancing and it is quite acceptable to seek competitive quotations. The conveyance is a one off task with a clear beginning and end. It differs from the accountant's task which is likely to be more on-going and therefore continuity becomes more important. All solicitors and accountants have a **duty of care** to their clients which some perform in a more positive way than others.

Costing the services of your agent

If a business transfer or local estate agent is used then his fees have to be added into the equation, too. These fees vary but are usually between about 3% and 5% of the contract price, with a minimum amount written in. Other terms may be offered by way of a lower fee for sole selling rights, or when you pay for or make a contribution towards the advertising costs (for more detail see Chapter 4 under the heading **Advertising through a business transfer agent** page 69). All agents are required to state their terms of business on their first contact with potential clients and you should insist on being told.

Negotiating over the landlord's legal fees
A cost which is at times overlooked and can be difficult to assess is the landlord's legal fees for preparing the **licence to assign** for a leasehold property. This document is the landlord's formal approval that the purchaser of the business can become his lessee or tenant.

- As a general rule for sales involving **industrial units** this cost is paid by the purchaser and for sales of **retail shop units** the cost is paid by you.

However, the issue of who pays often becomes part of the negotiations for sale. If agreement cannot be reached a compromise is made and the cost shared between the parties. You should settle this with your purchaser at an early stage — if it is left it can lead to difficulties later. A mention on the sales details can often forestall any arguments or discussion.

Costing normal home sale/purchase fees
Where the sale of your living accommodation is involved there are all the normal costs associated with moving house: removal costs, survey charges, loan arrangement fees, solicitor's expenses, stamp duty and so on. Up-to-date detailed information and cost guidance for house purchase is readily available over the counter from most building societies and banks.

Finding the money to pay the costs of sale
If you are in any doubt as to the likely costs then you must ask.

If you are in any doubt as to which expenses can be allowed against the business profits then you must ask.

If you are in any doubt as to what can be reimbursed by the Inland Revenue or the Customs and Excise you must ask.

SUMMARY

This may be the first and only time you are involved in the sale of a business. In this chapter the items which need attention after you have taken your decision to sell have been discussed. These have been looked at under the headings of timing, accounts, property, business

What will it cost to sell?

	Circle
Have you asked your accountant about his fees?	Yes/No
Will you be liable for Capital Gains Tax?	Yes/No
Have you assessed all other tax liabilities?	Yes/No
Have you checked what can be charged against your profits?	Yes/No
Can you reclaim VAT on selling fees?	Yes/No
Have you checked the finance agreements for repayment fees?	Yes/No
Have you asked how much your agent will charge?	Yes/No
Have you asked how much your solicitor will charge?	Yes/No
Have you allowed for your landlord's legal costs?	Yes/No
Have you had quotations for removal costs?	Yes/No
Have you estimated your resettling costs in your new home?	Yes/No
Have you made allowance for emergencies?	Yes/No

Fig. 7. Estimating the costs of sale.

unit, fixtures, fittings and equipment and costs. The work of preparing to sell your business may appear unduly long and tiresome but the time and effort you spend planning could prove very worthwhile. It may well make the difference between a relaxed and trouble free transaction and a sale which is long drawn out, fraught with difficulties and anxieties.

Knowledge of the costs and the likely final net figures provides an assurance and is essential information for you to have during any subsequent negotiations. What has yet to be considered is the detail of the asking price and the marketing of your business.

CASE STUDIES

Chris and Joan get down to business

While waiting for his advertisement to appear Chris takes out his file and checks that he has all the documents he thinks he will need. He goes so far as to compile a list of the equipment and get copies ready for the viewers. Joan realises the importance of giving a good impression and nags Matthew to paint the woodwork in the shop.

Chris goes to his bank and is told by the manager that he is becoming concerned about the overdraft and is considering reducing the facility. Chris is relieved that he has taken the initiative by deciding to place the fish and chip business on the market. The bank manager is also relieved to see that some action has been taken before he has had to exert pressure.

Mabel muddles along

Mabel realises she ought to find her accounts and looks for them in a dilatory manner among old piles of brown paper envelopes. She finds the accounts relating to four years ago and decides that they will just have to do for anyone wanting figures. She asks her nieces and nephews if, when the time comes to move, they will help. To which they reply, 'Yes, if we have time'. There does not seem to Mabel that there is much else she can do in preparation and decides that all the viewers will have to take her as she is. When she has a moment on her half day she does make an effort to trim the hedge instead of working on her latest tapestry.

Brian rushes into the task

Brian throws himself into doing more building work round the property. Half completed projects are worked on, new projects are started and the final decorating is neglected. Jill is annoyed because she knows what should have priority. Brian ignores everything she says — he feels he knows better. Jill struggles with the kennels accounts because she thinks they might be needed. To add to their troubles Sue starts to show signs of being very unhappy at the village school.

POINTS FOR DISCUSSION

1. Which activities are being tackled in the right way by our three business owners?

2. What key aspects of your present life will you be giving up when you sell your business?

3. In what ways have you not been totally honest with yourself about your motives for selling?

4. How much is it going to cost you to sell your business and move house?

Are you ready to sell?

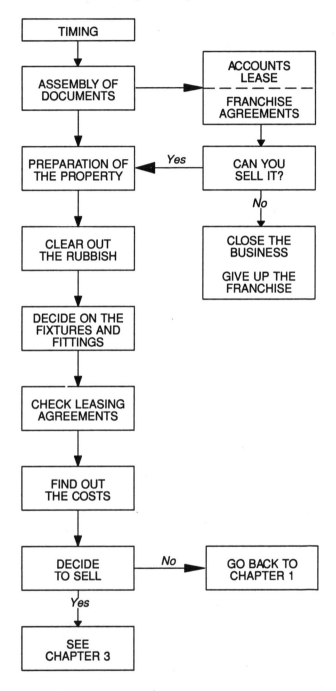

Fig. 8. Preparing to sell

3
Placing Your Business
on the Market

WHAT THIS CHAPTER WILL TELL YOU

In the process of reaching the decision to sell or otherwise dispose of
your business, you will have examined your reasons, talked it over
with your family, and possibly with advisers. You will have prepared
the property and the business for sale. You know what has to be
achieved, the likely costs involved and probably have a notion as to
what to do after selling.

In this chapter the process of placing your business on the market
will be discussed and you will now become involved with selling the
business alone or in partnership with agents.

ARRIVING AT THE ASKING PRICE

This is one of the most important single decisions to be taken and
there are several methods of finding an appropriate price. The
separate parts which make up the value were discussed in Chapter 1
but now you need to decide on a marketing strategy – and price –
which will attract potential purchasers to come and see your business.
You will be concerned not to pitch the asking price too low such that
you are giving the business away, nor to make it so high that there is
absolutely no response.

The wrong approach
The wrong approach is to take the price you paid, plus the associated
costs, plus the costs of any improvements, plus a percentage to cover
inflation — and call this the asking price. This will most likely produce a
figure which fails to relate to an appropriate marketing value.

The right approach
There are several more appropriate ways in which to reach a

reasonable market value.

Listening to friends
Note the price achieved by friends in the area who may have sold their businesses recently and try to relate what you have to sell with their businesses. This can be difficult because every business is so different. Friends may be reluctant to tell you how much they received for their businesses and you may only be able to gather the information through gossip or hearsay. Although such figures may be wildly inaccurate they may give some guidance.

Analysing advertisements for similar businesses
Read 'businesses for sale' advertisements and make comparisons. You may even consider asking for sales details to give you a more detailed comparison than can be made from the data in a small press advertisement.

The price for which the business is advertised is a marketing price and you will have no information as to how this price was arrived at, the level of genuine response nor the actual figure for which the business is sold.

The other danger is that in common with most people you may compare your business to one which is better than yours. The result is that you do not compare like with like.

Objectively only an outsider who looks at both businesses can make such a comparison fairly. For example, the comparison may be between a business with a quarter acre garden with another with a small paddock. You may consider the attractiveness of a large cultivated garden equates with a small paddock for a child's pony. However the market may well place a higher value on the paddock than the garden.

This method, although likely to prove more accurate than using friends, is likely to set the asking price a little too high and fail to attract the appropriate people.

Asking the opinion of your accountant
This also can be a guide but your accountant may never have seen your business, property or its location. His knowledge and experience may be limited to seeing the accounts of many small businesses and their final selling price. He may not have any experience of valuing a business and property together from a marketing viewpoint. He may be unaware of local conditions and the opportunities or otherwise for growth. Generally, and quite reasonably, an accountant will value the business according to the historical trading and profitability. He may be unduly

influenced by the balance sheet or he may be more used to considering business values from the standpoint of purchasers once a price has been agreed. He may be unaware of the value of exclusive agencies for products granted to that business in preference to its competitors.

Nevertheless his advice does provide an independent professional opinion. He can evaluate the business accounts by looking at them through the eyes of an accountant acting for a purchaser. He can highlight their strengths and weaknesses.

Working to a hunch
This method is completely haphazard and totally lacks research or logic. Surprisingly it may prove reasonably correct as long as you do nothing to inflate your original idea. It can be particularly useful when first discussing a marketing price, provided you are prepared not to stick to the precise figures dogmatically. It can provide a comparison for the figures produced by other methods.

Asking for an informed professional opinion
The income of a business transfer agent depends on selling businesses, so he has a vested interest in giving sound advice.

The business transfer agent provides a service for businesses similar to that provided for home owners by estate agents. Some owners are suspicious of prices suggested by agents and think that they will either unduly inflate them (to obtain instructions) or deflate them (to obtain a quick sale). Reputable business transfer agents will do neither. They will give their opinion based on recent sales, on the success of the business, the value of the property and the general activity of the market.

You could ask the opinion of more than one agent and ask each one to explain his reasoning.

COMING TO YOUR FINAL CONCLUSIONS

Your asking price must not be so unrealistic that when first compared with others it looks so out of line that nobody will even enquire. It is accepted that an asking price will be slightly inflated to allow room for negotiation, but too much inflation will deter enquiries.

The first presentation of the business on the market is the most important and the most likely to awaken interest. An asking price which is in dream land therefore needs to be avoided at all costs because no serious purchaser will reply. Testing the market at a very high price is a waste of everyone's time, money and effort. The decision is complicated by the fact that it is easier to reduce your asking price than to raise it.

What price should we ask?	
	Circle
Can my friends help?	Yes/No
Can other advertisements help?	Yes/No
Can my accountant help?	Yes/No
Can a business transfer agent help?	Yes/No
Can my hunch help?	Yes/No
Have I made my own decision?	Yes/No

Fig. 9. Arriving at an asking price.

If you use several or all of the above methods you should find yourself coming to an informed decision. There will always be a risk that market forces will catch you out but that applies to all aspects of business. You have to listen to and evaluate all the advice received and settle for a figure which seems reasonably attractive and yet allows scope for negotiation. Don't let others take this decision for you; you could come to regret it.

USING A BUSINESS TRANSFER AGENT

Business transfer agents are most active in the small family business community although at times they are involved with larger concerns.

The agent has a duty to negotiate the best possible price for his client who is usually the vendor. He is controlled by the same legislation as that governing estate agents. A business transfer agent is frequently the key to a successful sale and the services provided by a good agent can be invaluable.

- A good agent, as well as putting his expertise and experience at your disposal, takes over from you most of the work and effort of selling.

- The agent allows you to concentrate on your business and maintain its profitability without the distraction of placing advertisements, taking phone calls discreetly, despatching sales details, correspondence and so on.

- The day to day anxiety of selling, responding to and chasing enquirers is left to people for whom this is their primary task.

There is a choice of agents and a personal recommendation from your accountant, solicitor or friend may be helpful in the selection. Some agents advertise their services in trade, local or national press; others mailshot businesses whilst others will even canvass by telephone. Some agents specialise in one type of business, for example fish and chip shops, licensed premises, post offices and so on. Other agents handle all trades. Yet others work partly as estate agents and partly as business transfer agents. The vital ingredient is that your agent is active on your behalf and the advice given in all respects is sound and useful.

Getting an initial opinion

More than one agent can be called in and asked for their opinion of a realistic marketing price. Some make a charge for this service, others see the initial visit as an opportunity to promote their services, and will give advice without charge. To avoid nasty surprises you will need to ask, when telephoning, if the agent makes a fee for viewing and valuing your business.

What the agent does

In essence the work of a business transfer agent is similar to the work of an estate agent, except that the business transfer agent needs a broad knowledge of different types of businesses and to understand the meaning of trading figures. The business transfer agent will visit the business, provide an opinion of a realistic asking price, prepare sales details, advertise the business, negotiate a price with prospective purchasers, deal with any difficulties and generally see the sale through to completion. The agent is able to provide much assistance to both you and the purchaser because he is in regular contact with finance brokers, surveyors, accountants, solicitors and stock valuers.

He has experience of handling a number of sales each year. He can give advice, nudge all parties and their advisers into action, make recommendations and sort out apparently intractable problems. A good agent will know at all times the precise point any negotiation has reached, anticipate likely difficulties and deal with them before they grow and eclipse the sale.

The agent is uniquely placed because he is the only party able to speak direct with both sets of solicitors. Your purchaser's solicitor will not usually speak direct with you but only pass messages to you through your solicitor. A good agent is able to filter out anger or frustration between anxious people and quietly absorb abuse. He can give confidence to a nervous purchaser by providing local information, knowledge and introductions to solicitors, financial advisers, accountants, surveyors and so on. He is able to lessen your concerns as to whether the purchaser is serious.

Throughout the sale the business transfer agent knows that his primary duty is to you and he has to obtain the best possible price for your business. It is in your interest to work closely with your agent and together to seek to make a trouble free sale. It is in your best interest always to tell your agent about any changes in your business or business circumstances. Giving misleading information will make the conduct of any sale correspondingly more difficult and making false statements is a criminal offence under the **1991 Property Misdescriptions Act.**

Preparing for the agent's visit

Preparing documents for the agent
During his visit, the agent will view the property and seek to understand the workings and particular activity of the business. He will ask to see your most recent two or three years' trading accounts and to view bookkeeping evidence of the current year's trading. The latter can be your VAT return figures, daily takings records, purchase and sales ledger entries and so on. When a business is operated from leasehold premises then you should have available a copy of the lease for his inspection.

Without these papers the agent's visit will be of limited use. He may even refuse to act for you until the information and documents are produced. If the sales figures are with your accountant, and the annual accounts are in the course of preparation, then you should postpone any meeting with an agent. The ideal time for you to call him in is immediately you receive your latest annual accounts; he will have the latest trading figures and you will have been able to discuss any tax implications with your accountant.

Preparing other information
The agent will seek to learn as much as possible about your business. The better he is informed the more help he can be. He will ask about (and wherever possible ask to see) the terms of any lease or lease/purchase agreements, and planning permissions. He will ask about staff, wages, opening hours, business rates, stock values, licences, and business activity in the area. A good agent will then give an assessment of a realistic market value for your business. You can then decide whether to try to sell the business, to continue trading and hope for a rise in business values, or even to close it down.

In most cases it is the agent who takes the risk and invests his money to find a purchaser. (Occasionally a business transfer agent is

Which business transfer agent should we use?	
Where can you seek an agent?	
Through a friend	_____
Through your accountant	_____
From *Yellow Pages*	_____
From a mailshot received	_____
From a newspaper advertisement	_____
From a trade journal	_____
Is he familiar with your trade?	Yes/No
Does he advertise widely?	Yes/No
Does he charge for valuing?	Yes/No
Is he enthusiastic and eager to make a sale?	Yes/No
Are his fees competitive?	Yes/No
Do you have confidence in his ability?	Yes/No
Is his agent's agreement too prohibitive?	Yes/No
Can you work with him?	Yes/No

Fig. 10. Choosing your business transfer agent.

commissioned to find a particular business for an eager purchaser and the purchaser pays for the agent's services.) If vital information is withheld, or the agent considers that the asking price you are insisting upon is unrealistic, he may refuse to act for you.

Making time
The time needed by an agent for his initial visit varies widely according to the type of business and its complexity. It may help to give examples.

- For a freehold family run retail store with living accommodation at least two hours should be set aside. The agent has to take in a great deal of detail and you will want to be reassured that this particular agent is enthusiastic and likely to be effective in obtaining a satisfactory purchaser.

- A longer period is needed for a business which is unusual in its application, or manufacturing.

- A whole morning or afternoon may be needed for a medium sized hotel, for example.

- A leasehold lock-up business in a parade of shops on an estate could probably take up to one and a half hours.

Understanding different agency agreements

Most business transfer agents will ask you to sign an **agency agreement** before they will prepare sales details or advertise your business for sale. You should be given your own copy when you sign to keep for reference.

- As with all legal documents you must read and understand the agreement before signing.

If you have any doubts then ask for an explanation. If you are not satisfied ask for the explanation in writing, and if you still have doubts either do not sign with that agent or consult your solicitor. If a dispute gets to court the judge will assume that since you are in business you are quite well aware of the need to read and understand agreements before signing. Lack of knowledge of what has been stated is seldom accepted by courts as an argument and you may well find the court unsympathetic to your viewpoint.

'No sale, no fee'

Most agreements are on a 'no sale no fee' basis, although there are variations — particularly in respect of contributions by you towards advertising. If this type of agreement is being offered then you can ask for invoices or statements detailing the advertisements which have been placed, and only reimburse the agent against those invoices. An advertising budget may be agreed in advance; you may wish to become involved in planning the advertisements and the media to be used. A blanket sum paid to the agent for advertising could lead to abuse by an unscrupulous agent, especially if a purchaser is found from existing registers or from the first advertisement placed.

Three types of agency agreement

Agency agreements fall broadly into three categories.

Multiple agency agreements

These agreements usually say that the agent will only receive a fee when the buyer introduced by him completes the purchase. A multiple agency agreement permits you to appoint more than one agent and also to advertise and sell the business *yourself* without paying a fee to any agent.

In some agreements the terms include a clause stating that, if you change your mind and refuse to go through with the sale with a purchaser who is able to buy then a fee will be charged. Usually under multiple agency agreements you can remove your business from the agent without charge or penalty. As with all agreements you can arrange to contribute towards the cost of advertising in return for a lower fee.

Sole agency agreements with sole selling rights
These agreements are more complex. In return for a reduced fee you agree to pay the agent *however* the purchaser is found. The fee will be due *even if you find your own purchaser* and the agent plays no part in the transaction.

Since the agent is assured of his fee and there is no competition from others, the sole agent with sole selling rights should be more aggressive in marketing your business than would normally be the case. You need to question the agent accordingly.

Every sole agency agreement should state a time limit (usually between three and six months) for the agreement to be enforceable and state what happens at the expiry of the time limit. If these points are not covered then do insist on a full explanation in writing before you sign. You should press for and must have the full terms of this agreement in writing before you agree to his appointment. Usually the all important date applied to a sole agency sale is the date the purchaser was introduced and viewed the business and not the date of completion of the sale.

The sole agency agreement is restrictive but does have other advantages to which you may give a high priority. Using only one agent should ensure that there is a greater level of confidentiality and no confusion as to which agent sent which viewer nor can there arise any dispute between agents as to who introduced the purchaser. On the other hand it does restrict you if you lose confidence in your agent and have to wait several months before being released from the agreement.

Sole agency agreements without sole selling rights
This type of agreement is similar to the one above, but if you find the purchaser yourself you will not be liable to pay any fee. If however during the period of the agreement the purchaser is introduced by another agent then you will be liable for a fee to both agents.

In some parts of the country multiple agency agreements predominate; in others sole agency agreements, with or without sole selling rights. Some agreements include advertising contributions; others do not.

Appointing the agent

The agent's visit can be quite lengthy because you will wish to discuss the use of photographs, the degree of confidentiality to be observed, viewing arrangements, presentation of the sales details, advertising arrangements, negotiating procedures, possibilities of making a sale, stock valuing and so on. You will have many questions to ask and require to be reassured of the agent's attitude towards your business.

If you are satisfied and sign an agreement then within a few days you should receive a copy of the **sales details** to read and check. Every item needs to be carefully scrutinised and your agent told at once of any inaccuracy or error. The importance of only presenting correct information cannot be over-emphasised, not only for legal reasons but also for effective marketing. Many prospective purchasers are put off if the sales details show up even quite small errors when the business is first viewed.

The need for accuracy is seen as so important that some agents will even ask you to sign a copy with any amendments before they will start to promote the sale. Inaccurate advertisements and sales details can lead to a criminal prosecution under the terms of the **1991 Property Misdescriptions Act**.

MAINTAINING CONFIDENTIALITY

You may well fear that the knowledge that your business is for sale will damage trade and upset staff but in practice this rarely presents too much of a problem. There is a conflict because you are not wishing to broadcast that your business is for sale whereas prospective purchasers will want to know that it is on the market.

Using photographs

Photographs on sales details and in advertisements may help attract potential purchasers, although often it is difficult to take a photograph which truly reflects the business premises and the property. Photographs also greatly increase the risk of the business being identified by staff and customers. Be careful, because if a photograph is later claimed to be too flattering, or is deliberately taken to cut out a detrimental feature such as chemical plant next door, then criminal proceedings can be instigated against you and your agent. On the other hand a poor photograph may not do justice to your business and discourage people from enquiring further.

Telling customers and staff of your intention to sell

Usually the most uncomfortable part for you when everybody knows of your intention to sell is the endless questioning from staff and customers about the progress of the sale. It is depressing to be questioned frequently by well-meaning people when in reality there is very little happening.

Between taking the decision to sell and the actual sale you will really need to concentrate on maintaining the business and planning your future. You will probably have all the anxieties you can handle comfortably without hourly and daily reminders from staff and customers. It is even more discomfiting when there are health or financial pressures.

You may have customers saying that they have seen your business up for sale when you have had no intention or plans to sell. Sometimes customers seem to sense that a sale is being planned or you may have been slightly incautious. If this occurs you can usually disarm the customer by a light and humorous remark which needs to be said so as not to embarrass. Alternatively you may be quite open with your customer and extract a promise from him to say nothing more until a sale is announced. The surest way to protect confidentiality is when all thought of it is banished from your own mind when you meet staff or customers, and when nobody at all is taken into your confidence. This may not prove easy but usually works.

In most ordinary retail circumstances, customers knowing the business is for sale has little effect on sales as long as the business remains well run. If your enthusiasm for the business is seen to be waning then sales may well fall away.

Key staff

Some businesses such as a beauty parlour or hair salon provide a very personal service where extra thought has to be given to confidentiality. Many clients go to the person who does their hair even when they change salons. If the business and staff change, customers may follow the individual hairdresser to another salon or move to another salon anyway, rather than risk being treated by a stranger.

Knowledge of an intention to sell may prove particularly unsettling for skilled staff. They may seek another employer or in the case of a hair stylist decide to rent a chair in another salon.

You have to choose whether to say nothing and wait until your staff find out or take them into your confidence. There is no hard and fast rule and much depends on the individuals involved. You may even decide to offer the business to one of your staff on special terms. There are many occasions when owners have been surprised to find that this has led to a successful outcome, particularly for leasehold lock-up businesses.

Timing your staff announcement
Always tell your staff as soon as contracts have been exchanged and tell them whether they will be declared redundant, or whether the new owner is able to offer them continued employment. If you decide to tell the staff of your plans then tell them all at the same time and keep them up-to-date with all major developments as a sale progresses.

Telling the local gossip and expecting the word to be passed around can backfire because the local gossip may prove surprisingly reticent and refrain from talking about your plans. If customers are going to be told then a small discreet notice can be placed in the shop or on the notice board.

Using 'for sale' boards

'For sale' sign boards are rarely used for on-going businesses as these offer a strong challenge to customers to flee to other suppliers rather than risk being let down. Boards are needed for the sale of empty business premises and can be effective in attracting potential purchasers. To market a business without being able to freely identify it does hinder the task of selling, but most serious enquirers appreciate the need and will respect your wishes.

Using box numbers

You may decide to advertise using a box number and try to sell the business without using an agent. Unfortunately many enquirers are reluctant to put pen to paper and prefer to know the name of the recipient before responding.

Using a friend

An alternative way to preserve a degree of confidentiality is to refer the enquirers to a friend who knows the business but lives a little distance away.

Using an agent

This is the most effective way of keeping your plans from staff and customers. You can expect a reputable agent not to pass on the fact that you have enquired about selling even though you do not appoint him or even request a visit. His livelihood depends on business sales and so he will want to respect your wishes and keep your goodwill. An agent who agrees to make every effort to maintain confidentiality until viewing appointments are made is usually the best solution.

How important is confidentiality?	
	Circle
Do you want to use a photograph?	Yes/No
Do you want to use a 'For Sale' board?	Yes/No
Do you want to use a box number?	Yes/No
Do you want to use a friend/relative?	Yes/No
Do you want to use a business transfer agent?	Yes/No
Do you want to inform your staff?	Now/later/ on exchange
Do you want to inform your customers?	Now/later/ on exchange

Fig. 11. Deciding on the level of confidentiality.

When the agent visits you can either arrange this when staff are not employed, outside working hours, or by telling them that you have asked for an insurance quotation.

Agents are often placed under much pressure to reveal the name and location of your business to casual enquirers. If you feel strongly you can test how well a particular agent respects your wishes for confidentiality before signing an agreement. When more than one agent is appointed then the risk of the loss of confidentiality is greatly increased. Even when every precaution is taken customers somehow find out; it would be unreasonable to expect your agent to tell lies to enquirers who have correctly guessed that your business is for sale.

You may ask that your intended sale is kept from a particular person eg an ex partner or special customer. This can be difficult because people will use false names or addresses belonging to relatives if they really want to know. They will make viewing appointments and then cancel them. As a sensible precaution you can ask your agent to refer the names of all local enquirers to you before sales details or any other information is sent to them.

PREPARING SALES DETAILS

Good sales details are vital. You must avoid negative words such as 'not', 'never' and 'no'. When the reader finds these words in sales details he switches off immediately and puts down the sales details and starts to read another.

The sales details are your showcase. Their purpose is to give an accurate reflection of your business and property in a way that will entice an enquirer to proceed further and make an appointment to view. The information is needed by a prospective purchaser so that he can discuss the business with his own accountant, friends or financial advisers. The information will also be needed to draw up a business plan. Therefore every item on the sales details must be factually accurate, clear and easy to read.

Each individual will look at the sales details from a base of his own limitations, preferences and prejudices. When preparing the details, do use simple straightforward English and avoid slang or jargon. Take care with the presentation; too many words can prove as harmful as too few.

The prospective purchaser will be looking at a number of sales details and will not bother with any which are tedious to read. Too many superlatives will not be believed (even when true) and a word picture has to be put together which an average person will consider fair. The facts must be correctly stated and up-to-date. The presentation must be appealing. Poor spelling, untidy layout and faint photocopies betoken a slovenly attitude and an unattractive business. The purchaser will be influenced by the presentation.

When a prospective purchaser receives a sheaf of sales details you will want your business to stand out. A photograph of a snow filled garden received in midsummer tells its own story. Preparing good sales details is not an easy task and so part of your assessment of an agent is to look at other sales details prepared by him. It is worth taking the time and trouble to prepare a comprehensive and presentable information package about your business.

The information needs to be updated and amended whenever any changes occur to the business, trading pattern, fixtures, fittings, equipment, rates, rent and so on. A good typewriter or word processor can work wonders and there is no excuse with modern copiers readily available, for sales details to be presented in a scruffy manner. Giving the business a good image by a smart presentation on paper and so creating an excellent impression can only increase the chances of purchasers picking out your business from many others.

- The sales details are virtually the only selling tool you have after the advertisement to encourage the purchaser to step your way.

Choosing what to include

Describing the location
An indication of where the business is situated can often be provided without giving the exact address. For instance is it in a market town, village or city, is it on a main road, in a shopping precinct or on an

industrial estate, is it in East Anglia, North Wales or Scotland?

Describing the premises
Give an outline of the size, type and age of the property, retail sales area, manufacturing, preparation and stock areas, customer parking, and general condition.

Describing the living accommodation
State the number of bedrooms, toilets, living rooms with sizes, whether there is a garden, sheds, garage or other amenities.

Listing the fixtures, fittings and equipment
Provide a provisional list of fixtures, fittings, tools and equipment, all of which are included in the sale whether they are owned, on lease or lease/purchase. Optional extras such as a vehicle can be mentioned.

Giving basic sales and gross profit figures
This is a very important section because a purchaser will judge whether to proceed further or leave the business alone on the basis of these figures. As a minimum, state the **sales** and **gross profit** figures for the last year, saying whether the figures include or exclude VAT. Tell them about the previous year's trading and perhaps include a realistic projection for the current year and the expected earnings.

The figures need to be verifiable because most serious purchasers will wish to check by inspection of the accounts or VAT returns. You will probably hesitate to mention any additional income or sales which have not been included in the official trading accounts; in any case financial advisers to the purchaser will ignore such income. Such information could find its way to the Customs and Excise or Tax Inspectors who could ask many awkward questions!

Detailing the terms of the lease and the rent
Tell the purchaser the type of lease, its length, the rent and any particular restrictions. It will destroy credibility if you say it is a full repairing lease when in fact it is later found to be an internal repairing lease.

Stating opening times, staff numbers and wages
These will vary from one owner to another. It is helpful to a purchaser to know how much staff you use to run the business to achieve the stated sales figures.

Stating business rates and council tax
Knowledge of the rateable value and the business rates payable for

the year is important to the purchaser. Where there is accommodation attached many purchasers will wish to know the council tax band into which the property has been placed and the amount of tax payable for the year.

Estimating the stock value
The value of stock held will vary greatly according to the type of business and time of year. For a garden centre, toy shop, holiday business or gift shop the value of the stock which is held and essential to the profitability of the business will fluctuate widely during the year. Stocks in other businesses do not fluctuate so greatly. The purchaser has to know the funds needed to stock the business normally and those needed to carry the business through peak periods so that he can arrange finance from the outset.

There are times when the stock value is greater than the market value of the business. For instance a lock-up hardware store may carry stock to the value of £20,000 and the market value of the business may be only £15,000. In other businesses the stock value can be quite nominal, as in a travel agency business, although care has to be taken over any advance booking deposits and credits.

Stating the asking price
A clear statement of your asking price is essential and also what is included or excluded in the price. Surprisingly some sales details say 'an offer between £30,000 and £40,000 will be considered' in the belief that this will be an extra attraction. It would be a very strange purchaser who would value the business for more than £30,000. Many will offer less. Some sales details do not give a figure at all and the poor purchaser is left to guess if the business is for sale at £20,000 or £50,000.

State a value for your business and communicate this to the prospective purchaser from the outset. In most cases the purchaser will decide what he considers a fair price, bearing in mind your figure, and make an offer. Without your figure he has very little idea of your expectations and the sale takes more the form of an auction with a hidden reserve price.

Stating the viewing arrangements
These need to be clear and easy to find on the page. Failure to give an accurate telephone number is a disaster and you need to check and double check this. Viewing arrangements are sometimes shown at the top and the bottom of the sheet. You need to check that your advertisement has appeared correctly and ensure that there is someone available to take the calls. Answerphones are very much second best and

if nobody is there to answer the purchaser will go elsewhere.

Giving that little bit extra
A purchaser may find it helpful to have some information on schools, local amenities, local community and so on. Simple travel directions can be of great assistance in rural areas when confidentiality is not an issue.

When you receive copies of the details prepared by your agent look at them closely as if through the eyes of a prospective purchaser. If you are not satisfied, say so. After all, you have the most at stake and it is in your own interest to ensure that the best presentation is made of your assets. When giving room sizes give the larger measurement first and remember to be positive.

SUMMARY

The main considerations have been discussed for settling on an appropriate marketing price and placing the business on the market. The work and help available from business transfer agents has been considered together with different types of agency agreements. The reasons for maintaining confidentiality, use of sign boards and photographs and the preparation of sales details have been looked at in detail.

CASE STUDIES

Chris and Joan
After the failure of the local advertisement, the shock about the terms of the lease, and the customer comment, Chris and Joan are very cast down. When Chris had bought the business he had replied to a small advertisement in the local press. He had avoided agents because he was unsure of the integrity of business transfer agents and thought he would get a better deal from a private purchaser. He did not listen to advice and is now beginning to think that he paid an inflated price for the business.

Chris then remembers that when he became redundant and had the idea of buying his own business his employer's personnel officer referred him to *Dalton's Weekly*. For a second time Chris decides to go it alone to try to save fees and places an advertisement in *Dalton's Weekly* under a box number. Chris goes to a lot of trouble and expense to have printed twenty sets of glossy sales details which are full of information. There are no replies.

Mabel can't make up her mind

Mabel still does not know what to do about a price and cannot make up her mind. The situation drifts. The enquirer becomes so impatient that he begins to look elsewhere. When Mabel hears about this she tries to pull herself together and makes an appointment with her accountant. The accountant tells her bluntly that from a business point of view she ought to just close the business down, and either continue to live there or sell the property through an estate agent and look for something smaller.

Mabel is left still wondering what to do as she feels a commitment to the village to keep the Post Office and shop open. She has for years collected leaflets from business transfer agents which she has received through the post. She takes them all out and cannot decide so she phones the agents who advertise regularly in the local newspaper.

'Sell the kennels at any price!'

In a fit of temper Brian tells Jill to sell the place at any price. Jill places a display advertisement in several pet trade magazines and all the local newspapers. Customers telephone and say that as they are selling soon they would rather book their pets into other kennels this year. Several people telephone about the business who are primarily interested in the land; others start asking questions about trading figures and this year's bookings.

Jill does not know what to answer and as she has no real information to send, most of the potential purchasers just drift away. Jill dare not discuss the cost of the advertisements (£340) and the various phone calls with Brian and she is horrified to realise she is pregnant.

POINTS FOR DISCUSSION

1. In view of their personalities where have Chris and Joan, Mabel, Brian and Jill gone wrong?

2. How would you have avoided some of their troubles?

3. Describe to an outsider what you are trying to sell. How have you set the price and made your plans to achieve a sale?

CONFECTIONERY/TOBACCO/NEWS/GREETINGS CARDS

Mrs and Mrs Brown, Browns News, 23 PIER PARADE, PELLMELL BY SEA. Telephone (000) 123456.

LOCATION   We opened our profitable business in May 1990 in the central business area of the town which is close to the main dock passenger terminal and the sea front. We serve tourists, local businesses and the many casual passersby.

PREMISES   The shop area is 42 feet in depth by an average width of about 11 feet. The width does vary in different parts of the shop. We have 2 ice cream freezers and a slush machine on loan from suppliers, long magazine rack, greetings cards racks, double cool drinks cabinet, sandwich cabinet, serving counter with a Casio 4 department till and an illuminated cigarette display behind.
   At the rear of the shop is a shelved STOCKROOM (18 feet by 11 feet approx which includes along one wall a newspaper sorting counter. A TOILET is shared with the business who occupy the first floor.

TRADE   Our trading accounts show sales of £185,129 (excluding VAT) with a Gross Profit of £31,862 for our first 18 months trading up to 30th November 1991. Our cash book since shows sales, inclusive of VAT, of between £3400 and £3800 during the summer and between £2600 and £3400 during the winter. Our wholesale newsbill remains fairly constant through the year at around £750 per week and we do a small daily delivery to 18 business customers. We are considering applying for an off-licence.

LEASE   12 year internal repairing and insuring lease from February 1990. The rent is £7000 per year with 3 yearly reviews. The next review is not due until February 1996.

OPENING TIMES   7.30 to 5.30 pm Monday to Saturday. 8.45 to noon on Sunday. We open longer hours in the summer.

STAFF   We run the business ourselves with help from our son and daughter in law in the busier periods.

RATES   Rateable value £8534. The uniform business rates payable for 1993/94 including transitional relief was £3276.

STOCK   Our normal stock level is around £6,000 but does rise in the season to a peak of about £9,000.

ASKING PRICE   £36,000 LEASEHOLD, to include the Fixtures, the Fittings and the Equipment, and the Goodwill of the business. To view please always make a prior appointment to avoid embarrassment and to ensure that we can give you time to discuss the business thoroughly.

Date September 1993

Fig 12. Sales details sheet: leasehold example.

CITY SUBURB CAFE WITH 36 COVERS

FREEHOLD PROPERTY WITH THREE BEDROOM HOUSE

Mrs and Mrs Cook, Cookees Café, University Park Estate, Cley City. Telephone (000) 345678.

LOCATION   Our homely café is placed at the end of a small parade of shops which is situated between a large residential estate and the university with its open parklands. Many of the university staff work long hours and drop in for breakfast. We also serve local shoppers and workmen. There are no parking restrictions and customers rarely seem to have a problem. When the estate was built in 1975 many trees were planted which make it into a pleasant area.

PREMISES   The main café area is about 33 feet by 14½ feet with windows giving a view over the park. There are 10 tables and we use checkered cloths and all good stainless steel cutlery. We have a small extension of about 14½ feet by 6 feet and customers ladies and gents' TOILETS. A side door leads to a secluded lawned GARDEN between the property and the side road where we have placed TWO outside tables. At one end of the café there is our serving counter from where we hand out teas, coffees, cakes and snacks. Two register till.
The KITCHEN is about 18 feet by 14 feet and our equipment includes three microwaves, gas cooker, two Zanussi upright freezers, Indesit fridge, night storage heater, ice cream freezer (on loan from ice cream supplier), coffee machine (on loan from supplier), sink, hand basin and so on.

LIVING ACCOMMODATION   We live at the rear and above the business and over the years have made ourselves very comfortable. Most external windows have secondary double glazing fitted and we have an economical gas fired boiler. Gas fired heating. The upstairs rooms at the front have views of the park. On the ground floor we have a LOUNGE/DINING ROOM which is about 20³/₄ feet by 11³/₄ feet and a double glazed sliding patio door to our private GARDEN and south facing patio terrace. The fitted KITCHEN (about 10 feet by 9 feet) has a split level gas cooker. Understairs cupboard and staff TOILET.

FIRST FLOOR BEDROOMS
1. 14 feet by 9¼ feet.
2. 15 feet by 8³/₄ feet with parkland view. Built-in wardrobe.
3. 8½ feet by 8½ feet with parkland view. Built-in cupboard.
BATHROOM/WC. Airing cupboard. We have easy access to a large boarded loft storage area which is well insulated.
We rent a GARAGE in a block about 3 minutes walk away.

TRADE   Sales for the year ending 30th June 1993 were £47,222 with a Gross Profit of £29,424(62%). Sales for the previous year were £53,566 with a Gross Profit of £31,684(59%). Although our sales were a bit down over the 2 years we have raised our profitability from 59% to 62%. The business is open all year and we serve freshly cooked breakfasts, lunches, snacks, salads, home made cakes, soup and so on.

HOURS   6.30 am to 5pm all year. We do close Sundays.

STAFF   We employ up to 6 part time staff, many of whom are students. Our wage bill comes to about £80 per week. RATES Rateable value £2880. The uniform business rates payable for 1993/94 was £1198 and the living accommodation is in Council Tax Band D with £584 payable for 1993/94.

PRICE   £105,000 FREEHOLD, to include the Fixtures, the Fittings and the Equipment, and the Goodwill of the business. Stock is extra at valuation but this is usually very minimal and the maximum at any time will be about £300.
If these details arouse your interest at all then we hope that you will telephone immediately as we believe that our business is very profitable and we have always liked to live in good surroundings. Please do not come without ringing first because we are often very busy and unable to show you round.

Fig. 13. Sales details sheet: freehold example (1).

POST OFFICE/GENERAL STORES/OFF-LICENCE WITH 3 BEDROOM COTTAGE

Mrs and Mrs Stamp, Friendly Post Office Stores, Goffhead, South Upshire. Telephone: Goffhead 946.

LOCATION Our busy shop overlooks the green in this growing South Upshire village. On one side are the 19th century almshouses and on the other the church. The village is served by 2 pubs and a weekly fish and chip van. The mobile library stops outside the shop weekly. Since a by pass was built the village centre is again easily usable for the residents. The business has benefited.

PREMISES There are no parking restrictions and there is space at the front as well as space at the rear. The shop windows are shaded by awnings which give the opportunity for an attractive display. Inside the shop is L shaped with the maximum dimensions of 46 feet by 23 feet which provides about 600 square feet. Our equipment includes a 4 ft dairy deck, cool drinks cabinet, glass top chest freezer, ice cream freezer, fly killer, electronic scales, 4 department till, security mirrors, sales counter, Post Office kiosk, alarm systems, magazine racks, greeting card racks and so on.

The main shop STOCKROOM is about 18 feet by 12 feet and includes a secure cupboard, handbasin, cold meat slicer, scales, vegetable rack, sink and an oil fired boiler for the shop heating and hot water. STAFF TOILET.

OUTSIDE At the rear is a concreted area about 80 feet by 30 feet. We have arranged a number of plant containers to form a patio sitting out area. At the far end of which is a single brick GARAGE. For light storage we have erected a wooden garden shed.

LIVING ACCOMMODATION As we have inherited our parents' house a few doors down, we let the first floor accommodation on a short term tenancy. It is self contained and has its own access. The property will be offered with full vacant possession. Heating is by night storage units and coin meters are installed. Although it is in reasonable decorative order some areas would benefit from renovation to a new owner's taste.

The KITCHEN is about 12 feet by 6½ feet and includes a built-in cooker and larder cupboard. The LOUNGE is about 11½ feet by 11 feet. The BEDROOMS are about 13 feet by 11 feet, 9 feet by 5½ feet and 8 feet by 5½ feet. There is a BATHROOM (with shower fitting) and a separate TOILET.

TRADE The Post Office salary for our year to June 1993 was £12,000 and the shop sales were £262,935 with a Gross Profit of £32,629. Sales for the current year show an increase of 12% and we are expecting a substantial rise in salary from the Post Office. Our NET income we expect to be in the region of £30,000 before any finance charges.

OPENING TIMES 7.15 to 1pm 2pm to 6pm Monday, Tuesday, Thursday, Friday. 7.15 to 1pm Wednesday, Saturday and Sunday. We employ 3 part time assistants and pay about £140 in wages per week.

RATES Rateable value £4070. Uniform business rates payable £1694 in 1993/94. Council Tax band C. Amount payable £465.

STOCK To be sold separately at valuation. We estimate we hold about £10,000 normally.

PRICE £115,000 FREEHOLD, to include the Fixtures, the Fittings and the Equipment, and the Goodwill of the business.

When you telephone please can you only ask to speak to ourselves as staff sometimes answer the telephone. We will accept to see viewers by appointment.

Fig 14. Sales details sheet: freehold example (2).

Placing a business on the market

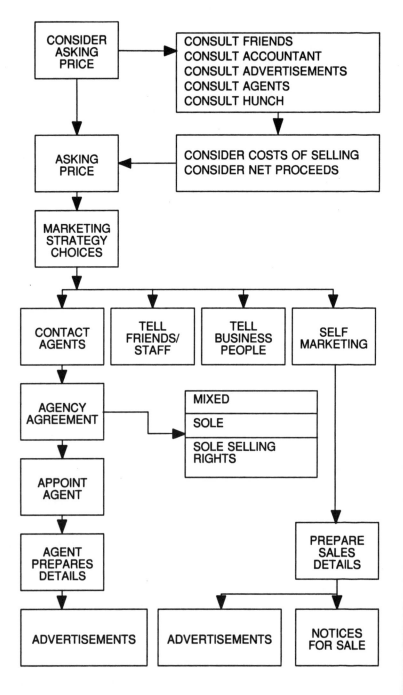

Fig. 16. Placing a business on the market.

4
Finding Interested Viewers

WHAT THIS CHAPTER WILL TELL YOU

This chapter explains various aspects of advertising and advertising media and ways to promote the sale of your business.

The purpose of advertising is to arouse the interest and curiosity of potential buyers sufficiently to make them pick up the telephone or write to ask for more information. The perfect advertisement is one which right away produces the buyer who can proceed and complete the purchase without delay. The sale of most businesses is the result of a specific advertisement for that business, so the choice of advertising media, the composition of the advertisement and how often it appears are all important. Therefore the advertising is of major importance.

ADVERTISING THROUGH A BUSINESS TRANSFER AGENT

Under most circumstances when you appoint an agent he will pay all the advertising costs as part of his overall service to you. As mentioned in Chapter 2 (**Estimating the selling costs**, page 40), it is considered usual in some areas of the UK for you to pay some or all the advertising costs in return for a lower fee when the business is sold. Elsewhere some agents, if they consider the marketing price insisted upon by you to be unreasonable, or if the business is very unusual, may ask for a contribution towards advertising costs.

Whenever advertising charges are agreed you should insist on reimbursing advertising costs against invoices, detailing where and when the advertisements were placed and their individual costs. A fixed sum for advertising leaves the arrangement open to abuse by the agent at your expense. He could try to collect money from all his clients and not spend it to promote the sale of their businesses.

If the agent insists that *you* pay the advertising costs, it shows that he thinks your business has only a limited possibility of selling at the price you are wanting. An agent who does not believe that your business is likely to sell may suggest to likely purchasers that they consider other businesses which he has on his register instead, because they offer better value. He will do this so that purchasers do not go to other agents in search of a business to buy. You may be able to judge what is happening by seeing how often he advertises your business.

If you are unsure about the effort which the agent will make on your behalf, then carefully review whether to appoint that particular agent or approach others (who might be more enthusiastic), reduce the asking price, or try to sell the business yourself.

An agent does ensure greater confidentiality by the advertisements appearing under his name only. He is also geared to reply promptly and efficiently to enquiries. You can even put this to the test by having a friend ring up and ask for the details. Your agent should also be offering your business to other clients who are replying to other advertisements. You have to rely on the agent's choice of media for the advertising but it is in his financial interest to select for maximum response.

DOING YOUR OWN ADVERTISING

These comments are designed to help those who are going to promote the sale of their own business. You may find them helpful even if you decide to rely upon an agent.

Choosing the right media

There is a wide choice of media in which to place advertisements for selling businesses. For some businesses it may be appropriate to select only one medium, for others a wider exposure may be advisable. The aim is to draw the attention to your business of all those who are looking. Advertising can become expensive, and so the aim is to avoid duplication without missing anybody.

Most classified advertising departments will give a precise quotation for any advertisement and they will claim they are the ideal medium. Budget carefully, because placing advertisements is so easy that a great deal of money can be spent carelessly. If your business is registered for VAT the VAT element can be reclaimed. Also, the expense of the advertising is a legitimate charge which may be set against profits.

Maintaining confidentiality

Unless you do not see this as a problem, confidentiality is a factor when considering how and where to advertise and how to deal with the enquirers.

The use of **box numbers** in advertising is an aid to confidentiality, but it inhibits many people from replying – either the anonymity of box numbers puts them off or they do not like writing letters. Some journals and newspapers have a policy of despatching box number replies only once a week, so delays can occur before you see the replies. Using a box number is a practical, if limited, alternative to using an agent.

Your accountant or solicitor may be willing to accept and process enquiries for your business but will charge for the service. A friend or relative may also be pressed into helping by providing a reply service and thereby easing the burden of unproductive telephone calls.

Drafting your advertising copy

The wording of your advertisements needs to be clear and precise. Statements must be accurate or you may find yourself committing an offence under the **1991 Property Misdescriptions Act**. When agents are appointed they take responsibility for the advertising copy, frequency and the choice of media; but this does not prevent you from expressing your opinion of which to use. It is in the agent's interest to try to maximise response by being knowledgeable about your business and you can help by ensuring that he learns the correct terminology for your trade.

Ideally the advertisement needs to attract only those who could be seriously interested and to eliminate the rest. Therefore as a minimum it needs to cover the following.

Describing your business

Generally, the first words or heading of the advertisement should state the nature of the business because this is what the purchaser will be seeking to know. He may skip over an advertisement which just starts 'interesting business' or 'profitable business for sale'.

If you own a very specialised business which can be readily recognised, you will need to give careful thought to attracting the right people to reply without losing confidentiality. For example, a plastic moulder whose prime business is supplying saddlers with camel saddle moulds is likely to have a one off business and be readily identifiable. An advertisement may therefore have to describe this business as 'a specialist plastic moulder for the craft leather industry'.

Stating the business product or service will reduce enquiries from people without the right background skills. To give some examples, a small family butchers must be run by somebody who is trained in cutting, preparing and presenting cooked and uncooked meats. On the other hand people with very different backgrounds can adapt to and be confident in running a general food store. Where you can provide training this can be stated.

Beginning words
Many publishers sort lineage advertisements into alphabetical order under each classification using the first letter of the heading. It is an advantage if the first letter of the heading is high up on the alphabet and your advertisement heads up the column. It is a disadvantage if you are sandwiched into the lower half of a long column of businesses for sale.

Describing the property
The reader must be told if the property is leasehold or freehold and whether there is living accommodation. Space needs to be used to include the number of bedrooms and to say if it is a flat or house. Many see a garden and garage as essential and will only consider properties with them. What is not mentioned will be assumed not to be there unless the advertisement is very brief indeed.

If your premises are leasehold, the length of the lease should be stated, together with any particularly favourable terms (for example the next rent review is six years away). The size of the retail sales area or manufacturing floor area may be given if particularly relevant.

Make it absolutely clear if there is no property involved, for example if your business is a mobile fresh fish sales round and you are including a suitably fitted out vehicle, or if your business is a newsround run from home.

Describing the business location
Some purchasers say they do not mind where the business is located; others are more specific. The important aspects are the part of the country in which the business is situated, ie whether the business is in East Anglia or London suburbs or if it can be relocated anywhere without detriment, and its immediate environment – village or town centre or Council estate and so on.

Stating sales figures and profits
People reading your advertisement will want an idea of the size of the business and its likely earnings. The sales figures rely heavily on the reader understanding and interpreting them correctly.

Some first-time buyers may not appreciate the difference between **gross profit** and **net profit** for example. Any figures you quote have to be capable of confirmation later by bookkeeping evidence, accounts, and other documentation. Stating bogus or exaggerated sales figures

Check your advertising copy

	Circle
Have you described your business accurately?	Yes/No
Have you carefully selected your beginning word?	Yes/No
Have you described your property accurately?	Yes/No
Have you described the location accurately?	Yes/No
Have you given accurate trading figures?	Yes/No
Have you included the asking price?	Yes/No
Have you put in a reference number?	Yes/No
Have you given contact information?	Yes/No
Is there anything else you need to say?	Yes/No

Fig. 16. A checklist of advertising copy.

to attract potential purchasers is illegal and futile. Vague words such as 'good profits' are a poor substitute for facts and figures even if these may be somewhat unpalatable. Most purchasers will ask for declared trading figures at a later stage anyway.

Giving the asking price
Don't be coy about the asking price. A potential purchaser needs to know if the business on offer is anywhere within his price range or aspirations. If a price is not quoted genuine buyers may be deterred. Even when properties are offered at auction a 'price guide' will be suggested by reputable auctioneers.

Using a reference number
Business transfer agents use reference numbers to identify individual businesses being advertised. You too can allocate a reference number so that you can tell which publication provides the greatest number of serious replies. This will be very useful when you come to consider repeat advertisements.

Giving contact information
Do not forget to include telephone number, address or box number because an advertisement which does not include a contact point will be a costly failure.

Giving consideration to additional padding
Other items may be included if they are thought to enhance the

Examples of advertising copy

Lineage or semi-display in Daltons Weekly
'Computer shop. Birmingham area. Detailed computer knowledge not essential. 1993 sales £452,671. Gross profit £91,819. Income @ £40,000. 20 year lease. Rent £9,500 per year. Next review 1998. Price £45,000 (plus stock). Telephone evenings only 021 123 6789'

'Country general store, village Post Office & gifts. 3 bedroom house facing village green. Garden & garage. UPVC glazing. Pennine walking centre. Post Office salary £9,250. Shop sales £500 to £2500 per week according to season. Average £1750 (ex VAT). Gross Profit 21%. £145,000 Freehold. Box No...'

Lineáge or semi-display in trade magazine
'Birmingham area retail computer business. Apple, Acorn and Amstrad agencies with contracts with schools and local authority. 1993 sales £452,671. Gross Profit £91,819. Lock-up unit on 20 year lease. Rent only £9,500 per year with next review in 1998. £45,000 plus stock at around £35,000. Telephone JS at JS Accountants for more information. Telephone (021) 987 4321 quoting reference BS001.'

Lineage or semi-display in a local newspaper
'Attractive freehold village Post Office stores. Pennine area. Traditional stone 3 bedroom house, garden & garage. Faces the green. Double glazed. Post Office salary £9,250. Sales average £1750 (ex VAT) per week at 21% Gross Profit. The weekly takings vary between £500 and £2500 according to season. £145,000. Box No...'

Fig. 17. Examples of advertising copy.

number and quality of the replies. A too glowing advertisement for a low price can produce a 'there must be something wrong' message. The complete advertisement must make sense in the market place.

You can argue about the wording of advertisements for ever and everyone has their own opinion. The guiding rule is to provide helpful positive information which is accurate and appropriate for the media and your business. It is wasting everyone's time to attract people who have neither the financial resources, nor the interest, nor any essential skills in your trade.

Deciding where to advertise

So far the various possible advertising media have not been discussed. If you are not seen in the right market place then any money you spend elsewhere will be money wasted. Being in the right place is more important than cost. The cost is negligible in relation to the benefits accruing from a successful sale. Unsuccessful advertising will feel like money wasted and advertising should be thought of as high risk essential investment.

Too frequent exposure can be counterproductive, and too little makes it harder to find a satisfactory purchaser. There are advantages in daily repetition of the advertisement for a single business because the second insertion will encourage the wavering enquirer to make contact, as well as catch the attention of people who did not see the ad first time round. Several advertisements close together followed by a gap of a few weeks is often a very effective pattern.

How often will you advertise?

The first advertisement for the business tends to arouse the most interest, and so you may decide that this should be bigger than later advertisements in the same medium. As soon as possible after the advertisement has appeared the wording and layout need to be checked for errors, and mistakes taken up with the publishers. They may offer credit or a free entry in the next edition.

Following the appearance of each advertisement, try to keep a record of the number of replies. Only armed with this information can you take sensible readvertising decisions.

How much advertising will be required is impossible to judge for any business. You can decide how much after say the first £100 of your budget and once you have had the opportunity of reviewing the result.

As a result of the review any or all of the above might be altered before the next £100 is spent. A step-by-step review of the budget helps to stop costs getting out of hand.

Fending off the space sellers

After placing an advertisement in a trade magazine you will often receive telephone calls or correspondence from rival magazines trying to cajole an advertisement out of you. However tempting such offers may seem, each approach must be examined on its own merits, and not on the advice of the advertiser who initiates the contact. Such offers can quickly lead an incautious person to spend far more than allowed for in the budget.

Checking your advertisement	
	Circle
Have I exceeded my budget?	Yes/No
Have I recorded all the replies?	Yes/No
Am I satisfied with the response?	Yes/No
Have I reviewed the wording?	Yes/No
Have I reviewed the layout?	Yes/No
Have I reviewed the first word?	Yes/No
Have I omitted anything important?	Yes/No
Am I under the appropriate heading?	Yes/No
Have I chosen the best media?	Yes/No
Shall I repeat this advertisement?	Yes/No
If Yes	When?
If no, where else can I advertise?	____?

Fig. 18. Advertising checklist.

- Ask yourself: where would *you* look for an advertisement to buy a business such as yours?

You may also ask yourself where a prospective purchaser would look to find out about your business. The answer to the two questions may be the same but sometimes they are different. For example, you may go looking for businesses through the national newspapers whereas the right media for advertising your business may be in the trade press.

Using trade magazines and monthly journals
Most trade magazines carry a few ads of businesses for sale although these tend to be swamped by job or product advertisements. Advertising is relatively expensive; it is geared primarily to series products and services advertisements rather than businesses for sale. They attract replies from curious competitors rather than enquirers with a real interest in buying.

Trade magazines tend to lie around for some time in offices and public places and enquiries about a business may be received months later. Newspaper or weekly journals advertisements tend to have a very short useful life.

In a few instances the trade magazine is the normal and accepted medium and goes out to all members of the trade or trade association. Some professional institutes or highly skilled trades have their own circulations to individual members and list businesses and partnerships for sale. These are mostly the professions such as accountancy firms, solicitors, dental practices and so on.

Some journals cater for both the trade and the public and among these can be considered *Horse and Hound* and *Dog World*.

Another group consists of journals which circulate only to companies and have small individual subscription lists. Examples of these are *Estates Gazette*, *Croners* and various investment periodicals.

Many enquiries are likely to be from businesses seeking to invest in another outlet or branch.

Closing dates for acceptance of ads in monthly magazines are often two, three or even four weeks ahead of publication. This is a long run-in when selling a business because by then the need for the advertisement or the accuracy of your copy could change.

Identifying the right magazine
There are several checks you can make when trying to decide if a particular trade journal is likely to bring forth a purchaser.

Using an advertising agency
You can discuss the placing of the advertisement through an advertising agency (although most are unlikely to be interested in booking a single small advertisement for a one-off customer). However, if you use an agency regularly as part of your business it will probably be pleased to act. As usual, ask about the charges for any artwork and so on.

Researching trade directories
A good public library will obtain, or have available for reference, a directory of trade journals which lists all journals and their publishers. The directories give details of circulation, advertising costs and addresses of the classified advertisement departments. If you are unfamiliar with a particular magazine then most publishers will forward a back copy for you to inspect, a rate card and an advertiser's pack.

Analysing back copies
A careful analysis of the advertising in a back copy will suggest its appeal for selling businesses. For example the major business transfer agents will not waste money, time and effort in advertising in magazines which fail to produce buyers. When there are only a very

few businesses for sale, and it is not a journal in which you would have chosen to look for a business, then it is unlikely to be much use. However if the cost seems reasonable you could give it a try.

Some trade journals have become the main market place for businesses for sale for their trades. A close inspection of the advertisements will help you decide the wording and layout. Most serious purchasers will read the lineage advertisements in their search, as well as display advertisements, so you can save money in this way.

Discussing the advertisement with publishers
A telephone call to the 'classified section' of the publishers can help you to come to a decision, although the publisher has a strong vested interest in selling his advertising space. The staff will provide a comparison of costs for lineage, semi-display, use of box numbers and so on.

Using local and national newspapers
Newspapers reach a wider clientèle than trade magazines and catch the attention of people who may not have considered buying a business. Many buyers are entering the self-employed business market for the first time and begin their search by looking at the 'businesses for sale' ads in the daily press. Such buyers are often unaware of the specialist publications and look only in the local or national newspapers.

Just as you need to analyse each trade magazine so you need to look at the newspapers before taking the plunge. Take a commonsense approach. An advertisement for a lock-up business is likely to work better in a local newspaper than in a national one.

Some lock-up businesses are thought of as a secondary activity for the family rather than the main breadwinner. They are bought and sold almost casually because they change hands often for relatively small sums. Lock-up businesses are usually bought by local residents unless the purchaser is planning to move to the area for other reasons.

For a person in Manchester contemplating moving to Norfolk a business with accommodation attached will probably have more appeal because the problem of where to live is taken care of. Therefore it makes more sense to use local media for lock-up businesses and national media for businesses with accommodation. However this is by no means a hard and fast rule.

Paying for the advertisement
Most journals and newspapers will accept bookings for space over the telephone as long as the booking is confirmed in writing. Payment is

usually required in advance, by credit card or by the use of a proforma invoice.

Saving some of the expense
The cost of advertising in the national press is much higher than in the local press and many newspapers offer special deals which are worth checking out. For example an advertisement placed on three consecutive days may be charged at the price of two.

The effectiveness of a newspaper advertisement will last for only one or two days whereas advertisements in trade magazines have a longer useful life span.

Using specialist journals for business sales
The most well known and successful weekly publication is *Daltons Weekly*. This journal goes out of its way to promote the sale of retail and service businesses. It is particularly useful in that it is widely read by most serious prospective purchasers.

If your business is a small manufacturer it is not ideal but still worth considering. Copies of *Daltons Weekly* and similar publications even find their way abroad where they are read by expatriates considering returning to the UK. Telephone calls may be received from as far afield at California and India.

At regular intervals other publications are launched and distributed through newsagents. These can be considered but most are shortlived.

Conforming to the publisher's requirements
Some newspapers and journals follow a strict code about which advertisements they will accept and the copy has to conform to the house style and abbreviations. Whatever is submitted editors retain the right to amend although they rarely exercise it in businesses for sale advertisements.

All periodicals have to work to strict deadlines. All copy should be typewritten and laid out with clear instructions. Poorly handwritten copy gives the newspapers an excuse for rejecting any claims for compensation if the advertisement appears incorrectly.

Responding to enquiries
Unless a box number is used most initial enquiries will be by telephone. You may have to make special arrangements to answer the telephone and be very circumspect with your calls so as not to arouse the anxiety of staff or make them aware that your business is for sale.

Keep a notebook and pen by the telephone to take down names, addresses and telephone numbers efficiently. It is most irritating for a person who is making several calls to be greeted each time with 'just a moment while I get a pen' or 'sorry this pen never does write well'. The caller will be pleased and feel more welcome and secure if dealt with in a businesslike manner from the start. You will find it useful later to have taken notes of the conversations with times and dates. When you are running a busy shop it is easy to confuse messages and arrangements if you do not write them down immediately.

Answering the telephone
The importance of the first contact cannot be overstated. Much information can be gleaned from it because this is when the purchaser is least on his guard. He may be feeling quite timid, unsure what to ask and what he is letting himself in for. He may have read horror stories about people who have been conned.

First time purchasers will certainly lack confidence and seek reassurance from you that all is well and that his is a quite normal request and will be taken seriously.

Asking and replying to questions
All questions put to you have to be answered in full. Be prepared to discuss at length the good and less good points about your business from a positive standpoint.

- Unpleasant facts must not be hidden, with thought they can be presented in an acceptable way. For example if the business is in the middle of a Council estate you can reply, 'I am tired of living in this rough area where there is a lot of petty pilfering and I hope you can cope with that' or 'I have lived here for four years and with some adjustment I have learned to get on with all types on this Council estate and they all feel able to use the shop.' With thought you can express most negatives in a way which will not put people off.

- If you promise to send sales details or find out more information and telephone back, all such promises need to be kept even though you may not believe the person will take his enquiry further. The enquirer may have a friend or client who might be interested – don't risk choking off any possible purchaser.

- The enquirer needs to be told if there will be any delays in getting the information to him. Any lack of appropriate response may make the enquirer hesitate and pursue his search for a business elsewhere.

- Your aim is to make the enquirer feel comfortable and confident that the business is the one he wants above all the others. You have to make the enquirer feel that he is dealing with a reasonable person who is serious about selling, not somebody who is going to mess him around and change his mind later. Ideally the enquirer will convey a similar message to you. Whatever is done you must not put on an act because in any later meeting you will be found out. The purchaser will wonder what nasties you are hiding, and back off smartly.

- If the conversation is going smoothly you can ask whether the purchaser is able to proceed immediately or whether he has a property to sell first. It has to be said that you may not receive a truthful reply. It is certainly part of the responsibility of your agent to ask these and other questions on your behalf at this initial stage.

Following up the initial contact

Always use first class post. Sending second class is a false economy because it allows time for enthusiasm to cool.

When first talking you may be asked to supply a copy of your accounts. You may not wish to give them out to every casual enquirer. Make sure the sales details sheet includes sufficient trading and other information for an enquirer to decide if it is worth his time and effort to view.

Should the enquirer press the request for the accounts, he could be genuinely interested or simply curious. You will have to decide. The request may come from a person who has a long and tedious journey to view and seeing the accounts beforehand could be reasonable. On the other hand the request may come from a person who lives locally and therefore it might be just idle curiosity. If you do agree to the request, send photocopies which can be verified later if need be. Your originals are unlikely to be returned.

The use of television or local radio has not been discussed although for a very few businesses it could be tried. There is no magic formula better than a good dose of patience and commonsense.

SUMMARY

In this chapter we have examined the main media in which advertisements may be placed and the content of the advertisement. Finally some ideas about the most appropriate and positive responses towards enquirers have been suggested.

CASE STUDIES

Chris decides to advertise his shop for sale

Chris is in a situation he has not experienced before. He is baffled and for the moment cannot think what to do next. Turning over the pages of *Daltons Weekly* he notices a block advertisement with many fish and chip shops and on the spot decides to telephone the agent who is named. The agent immediately tells him that 'of course he can sell the business and will do so in a week.' Then he says, 'By the way what price are you asking?' Chris is suspicious and thinks that this is too good to be true – how can the agent possibly say he can sell the business in a week without even knowing the asking price or seeing the property? Chris thinks to enquire about selling fees and receives a very non-committal reply. At the end of the conversation Chris says he will ring back, but has no intention of doing so.

Now somewhat disgruntled, but seeing a possible way forward, Chris decides to talk to a local estate agent who is a regular customer. The estate agent tells Chris that he does not handle business sales himself and suggests that he tries a display advertisement in the trade journal. Chris thinks deeply about the wording and finally decides that he will reveal the turnover, the fact that the property is leasehold and has four bedrooms. He leaves out an asking price because he decides to try and obtain a free valuation from a business transfer agent recommended by the bank manager in the interim.

'Keep the post office,' says Mabel's agent

The agent calls on Mabel by appointment early one evening a little before closing. Mabel is pleased he is so prompt and he seems to grasp the position immediately.

The agent carefully inspects the property, measures all the rooms meticulously and makes copious notes. At the end he gives the same advice as Mabel's accountant which is that the sensible course is to close the shop. However, he suggests that the Post Office be retained on a part time basis and gives a marketing figure for the property, with the Post Office, which is only a little below Mabel's original vague notion of a price.

Mabel has not thought of this compromise and considers this the way ahead to solve all her problems. She promptly signs the agency agreement form on a sole selling rights basis. She fails to appreciate that she is now committed to an agent's fee even if her original enquirer buys her business and property.

Jill gives Brian some pause for thought

Jill plucks up her courage and tells Brian that she is pregnant and in the same breath the cost of the advertising. Brian goes quiet and to Jill's surprise is quite calm. Brian tells Jill that he has been very worried for some time about a large unpaid invoice and has been told that day that the cheque for the full amount is in the post.

After Sue has been put to bed they sit down together and study all the advertisements in the magazines and go through the replies to their own. Fortunately Jill has kept a note of telephone numbers. Brian impulsively reaches for the telephone and invites all the various enquirers to come to an open day at the kennels in two weeks' time. Brian promises Jill that he will arrange for some help to tidy the place up and he will now finish as many jobs as he can.

POINTS FOR DISCUSSION

1. Each of the business situations in our case studies has reached a crisis. Can you now foresee what crises you may need to resolve as you place your own business on the market?

2. What would you like to know when you are buying a business?

3. What appeals to you in advertisements and how would you like to be treated?

4. When preparing to sell your business what will you be looking for when an agent comes to see you?

How to Do Your Own Advertising
Michael Bennie

This book is for anyone who needs – or wants – to advertise effectively, but does not want to pay agency rates. Michael Bennie is Director of Studies at the Copywriting School. 'An absolute must for anyone running their own small business' *Great Ideas Newsletter.* 'Explains how to put together a simple yet successful advertisement or brochure with the minimum of outside help.' *First Voice (National Federation of Self Employed and Small Businesses).*

£7.99, 176pp illus. 0 7463 0579 6.
Please add postage & packing (UK £1 per copy.
Europe £2 per copy. World £3 per copy airmail.)
How To Books Ltd, Plymbridge House, Estover Road,
Plymouth PL6 7PZ, United Kingdom.
Tel: (01752) 695745. Fax: (01752) 695699. Telex: 45635.
Credit card orders may be faxed or phoned.

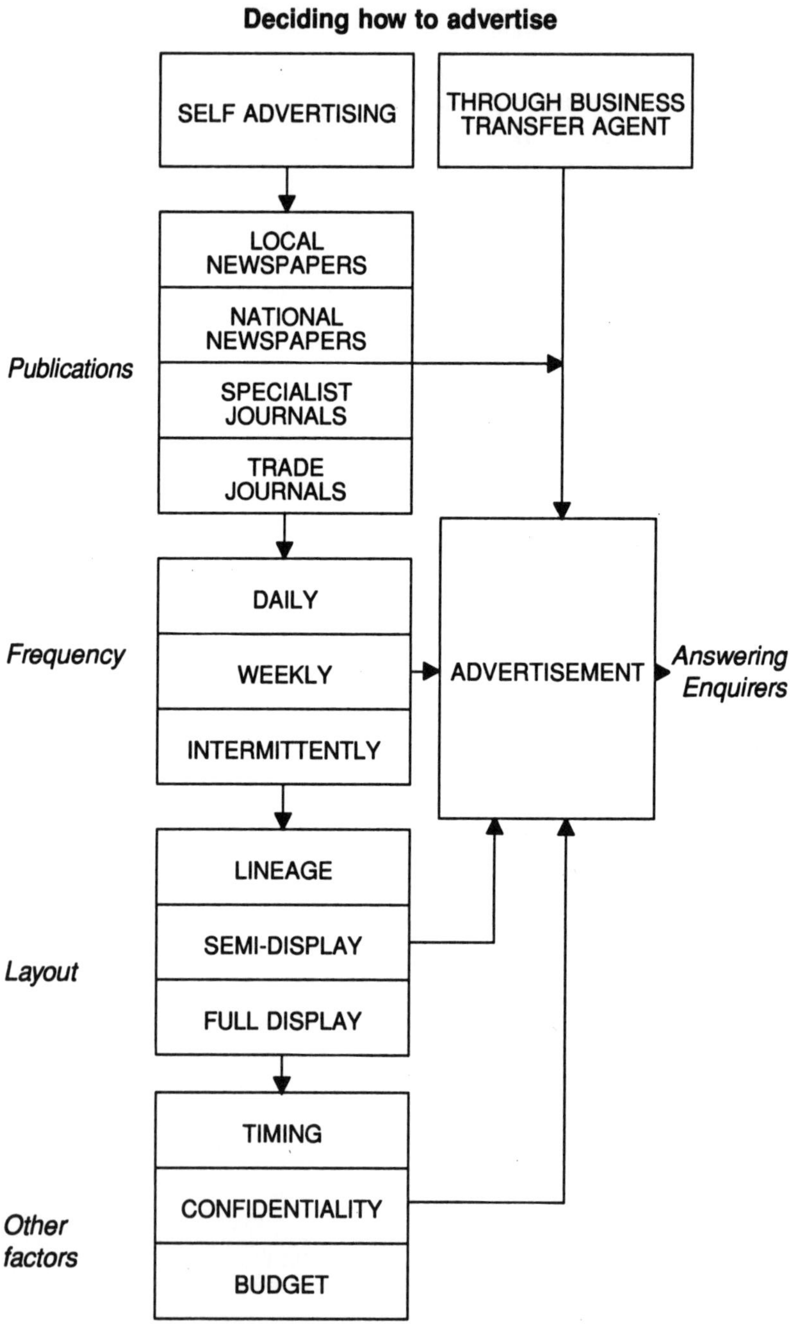

Deciding how to advertise

Fig. 19. Deciding about advertising.

5
Viewings and Negotiating

WHAT THIS CHAPTER WILL TELL YOU

In this chapter the actions required before, during and after the visit of potential purchasers will be considered. Business transfer agents do not normally accompany viewers. This makes it particularly important that you are alert and well prepared. The manner in which viewers are looked after and their first impressions can make the difference between a comfortable and amicable sale and a sale fraught with difficulties.

In the second part of the chapter the essential features of negotiating a business sale are described.

ARRANGING VIEWINGS

The object is to present and sell your business as a viable concern at a price acceptable to both parties.

Requests to view mostly follow quite soon after receipt of the sales details. However some people gather sales details at the time they put their own property on the market and refrain from following them up until their property is under offer.

Viewing should always be discouraged until the enquirer has received the sales details and has had a chance to read them. The viewing will then be more purposeful, and misunderstandings avoided, because the pertinent facts about the business have been written down and are not being conveyed by word of mouth.

There may be times when prospective purchasers hear about your business by accident when they are in the neighbourhood and call in on the off chance. Under these circumstances a copy of the sales details can be handed out or, if not immediately available, then forwarded.

As in all selling, the first impression becomes the lasting impression, so taking pains at the outset will improve the chance of

```
┌─────────────────────────────────────────────┐
│          HANDOUT NOTES FOR VIEWERS           │
│                                              │
│  Name of business.........................   │
│                                              │
│  Address of business......................   │
│                                              │
│  ..........................................  │
│                                              │
│  Name of owners...........................   │
│                                              │
│  Telephone number(s)......................   │
│                                              │
│  Nearest railway station..................   │
│                                              │
│  Bus service..............................   │
│                                              │
│  Primary schools..........................   │
│                                              │
│  Secondary schools........................   │
│                                              │
│  Public library (or mobile)...............   │
│                                              │
│  Medical centre...........................   │
│                                              │
│  Dental practice..........................   │
│                                              │
│  Police station...........................   │
│                                              │
│  Major shopping centre....................   │
│                                              │
│  Local leisure activities.................   │
│                                              │
│  Other....................................   │
│                                              │
│  ..........................................  │
│                                              │
└─────────────────────────────────────────────┘
```

Fig. 20. Handout notes for viewers.

making a sale. Not bothering to make your viewer feel that he is expected and welcome will make him feel less comfortable and you will not be making the most of your opportunity. Careful preparation is the key and it is now that your forethought and effort will pave the way towards a successful outcome.

Timing viewing appointments

You are probably very busy and free time is precious. Making time available to see your viewers can prove an irritant and such feelings need to be hidden. To maintain confidentiality in front of staff you can introduce the viewer as an acquaintance, a friend, or somebody who has been referred to you just to see how such a business as yours operates.

Allowing sufficient time
The viewing appointment should be made for when you have time to

show people round and answer their questions with the minimum of interruption. When agreeing the appointment allow at least an hour. Some viewings are over in ten minutes, others may last two hours. There is no rule nor is there a correlation between the time spent on the viewing and sales. Clearly, viewings at a small lock-up business are likely to be shorter than viewings on a lovely summer's day at a larger business which includes living accommodation and a large well stocked garden.

If the timing is difficult then seek an alternative. If this cannot be done without either postponing the viewing to a long time ahead or resorting to a 'we will contact you again' approach, then you will have to find some other way.

Accepting a viewer may mean altering your usual weekly pattern of work and disrupt staff. It will often be easier for you to alter your arrangements than for the viewer who may be snatching time off work or from his own business in order to see several businesses during one outing. It can become tiresome for you to be continually altering arrangements and fitting round responsible (or even irresponsible) viewers, but if you take too cavalier an attitude then opportunities for selling may be lost. The more seriously interested viewer will generally be prepared to be understanding as it is equally in his interest to make the most of any viewing opportunity. This applies particularly to a second visit.

Timing viewing appointments after opening hours

If an appointment is made for a lock-up business outside the normal opening times you can specify a precise period of time for the viewing to take place. If the time agreed is open ended you will be in a quandary – how long should you wait if your viewer does not show up soon after the agreed appointment time? You could agree with him beforehand to remain on the premises from say 6 pm to 7 pm unless he telephones.

Dealing with time wasters

It is difficult to eliminate time wasters or those with unrealistic expectations of what they can afford. A snap value judgment can often prove incorrect and so should be avoided.

Giving route directions

When the viewing appointment is made, give clear route directions with landmarks and exchange telephone numbers. Either party can then get in touch to postpone or alter the arrangements. There is no excuse for your viewer not turning up or getting a message to you but regrettably it does happen all too often, and you must be prepared for it. There are always people who will just drive past without stopping; or when their car breaks down the day before they will make no attempt to tell you or your agent. If you believed all the stories of car breakdowns there would seem to be very few reliable vehicles on our roads. You will certainly not feel very accommodating towards somebody who has let you down. But take care that just because one person does not arrive you do not take your frustrations out on the next. Treat viewing on its own merits.

Making overlapping appointments

There are differing views as to whether viewings should be allowed to overlap. There are advantages and disadvantages when viewers realise that others are sufficiently interested to view. Some people, seeing there may be competition are discouraged from trying to purchase. Others are spurred on to make up their minds more quickly.

Having two or more groups viewing at once will place a strain on your resources because each party will need the full attention of yourself or your partner as they are shown round and seek to discuss the business, local amenities and so on. On balance seeing more than a single set of viewers at once is best avoided, even when your business is closed to customers. Despite the best plans there are times when two parties coincide and having both around at once becomes unavoidable as one party may arrive late and the next arrives early. Turning people away will be taken as a hostile gesture wherever the fault lies so find a way round without giving offence. For example you can suggest a walk round the village or a visit to the church. You can sit one party down with a cup of tea, the local newspapers and amenity guides while the other is being attended to.

Making final preparations

Having sorted out the appointment, make the viewers feel they are expected. The business and property need to be tidy, family dogs and cats out of the way, stock tidy, and so on. On arrival the viewers need to be welcomed and greeted with a smile even if they are late, have three grubby grizzly children and a dog let out to run riot in the garden. Your viewer needs to feel that you are on top of the business and confident in its appeal.

If your presentation is generally sloppy and untidy then your viewer will be left with the impression of an uphill struggle to sort out your muddle and mess at the same time as taking over the business. The purchaser may well argue to himself that because of this mess the business is overpriced and his offer may reflect this judgment.

Assurances that the mess will be tidied before handover may not count for much, especially with an experienced person.

Do make sure that everything is ready in advance and everything which might be needed is to hand. Poor preparation is so common that if *you* prepare efficiently you will create an excellent impression and any negotiations are likely to take place in a more relaxed manner. Copies of the trading accounts for the last three years and more recent trading figures need to be ready as well as copies of leases, licences, lease/purchase agreements and so on. A prepared sheet listing local amenities can be most helpful (see page 86).

A poor impression will be created if you are asked for the trading and profit and loss account, only to have to dive through a heap of old brown paper envelopes stuck in the back of a filing cabinet before finding a tatty old copy of the accounts referring to four years ago. Muttered comments like 'I had them yesterday' do not help.

Showing people round

Most people prefer to look round the property before sitting down, inspecting the accounts and generally discussing the business and local amenities over a cup of tea or coffee. Other viewers simply take a quick glance round and then want to be on their way. You have no way of telling in advance.

Reacting to the viewers

Experienced business transfer agents will confirm that offers made *during* the first visit are seldom to be relied upon and are frequently withdrawn just as casually. Treat such offers with caution and avoid making promises that other offers will not be accepted. It is best to defer any acceptance and say that offers will only be considered when received through your agent. If an agent is not involved then say that you will let them know tomorrow. Either way this gives you time to discuss the implications of the offer among yourselves, with your financial advisers and with your agent. It gives time for the purchaser to have second thoughts and for your agent to check the purchaser's finances and see if the purchase depends on the sale of another property.

Viewers leave very differing impressions behind them. Some express tremendous enthusiasm at all the businesses they see even if they have no intention of proceeding further with any of them. Others give the impression of a complete lack of interest and yet are on the telephone to your agent next morning with a good offer. Wait for the evidence of a genuine offer before leaping to any conclusions about any particular viewer, however difficult it may be to control a surge of elation at the prospect of a sale.

```
┌─────────────────────────────────────────────────────┐
│                   Viewing notes                      │
│                                                      │
│  Time and date of viewing..........................  │
│  Name of viewers...................................  │
│  Address...........................................  │
│  .................................................   │
│  Telephone number .................................  │
│  Name of agent or source of viewer ................  │
│  Did they come on time? ................... Yes/No   │
│  Are they in a position to go ahead?......... Yes/No │
│  Comments and immediate impressions................  │
│  .................................................   │
│  .................................................   │
│  .................................................   │
│  .................................................   │
│  .................................................   │
│  .................................................   │
│  Actions which need to be taken, eg forwarding a copy of │
│  the accounts.....................................   │
│  .................................................   │
│  .................................................   │
└─────────────────────────────────────────────────────┘
```

Fig. 21. Example of notes following a viewing.

Making your notes

After each viewing you can make some notes to act as a reminder during any subsequent contact.

POST VIEWING ACTIONS AND RESPONSES

If you are not using an agent then a follow up phone call should be made within a few days to enquire if the viewer is really interested or not. If the viewer came through an agent then the agent will follow up the viewing and report back to you. Sometimes the reaction given to your agent is the complete opposite to the one shown to you. Rarely is it completely in accord; most viewers will be non-committal towards you and more forthcoming to the agent, which makes it difficult for you to judge them accurately.

Unfortunately agents often have to respond to comments such as 'I got the distinct impression that Mr Vendor does not really want to sell.' Whilst you clearly do not want to suggest that you are ready to sell at any price, going too far the other way can be just as harmful. Your agent can help the viewer through reassurance and advice if needed.

Often prospective purchasers will want to discuss the business with an experienced business person who has also seen the business. This may be a bank manager, accountant, friend or more experienced relative. At all such times the agent is a useful intermediary. If any copies of your accounts, agreements, lease and so on have been promised then your agent may be asked to supply them from documents held in his files. Promises to obtain and forward information should be fulfilled promptly, or if there is going to be a delay then your viewer needs to be told.

Comments made to you or your agent should be listened to carefully and put to good use with the next set of viewers. As the most successful sales occur when client and agent work as a team it often helps to exchange ideas after the visit of each potential purchaser.

Interpreting viewers' comments
These range anywhere from 'what a duff business' to an offer at the full price without quibble. In between are 'we have not yet talked about it', 'we have to make an appointment with our accountant/ bank manager', 'we must sell our house first before even considering which business to buy', 'we have a number of other businesses to see' and so on. Most of these replies mean that the viewer was not really interested but does not like to say so in a direct way.

When some further action has been initiated before the follow up contact, this can be taken as a positive sign of real interest. You can feel encouraged if the reactions to the viewing are 'we have made an appointment with our financial adviser on Tuesday', 'can you send a copy of the trading account and a clean copy of the sales details', 'we would like to arrange a second visit next weekend and suggest Sunday at about 3 pm', 'do you think we could be in by the beginning of the school year if we find a buyer for our house by June', 'we were going to telephone to ask what sort of offer to make', 'we would like to go further what is the next step' and so on.

Whenever there is the real chance of an offer being made, regular follow ups are essential. You and your agent need to make a diary note to follow up again after a second visit, or once the interested party has seen his bank or financial adviser. Stay in touch with every serious potential purchaser until an offer is made or until you and your agent become convinced that further discussion will be counter productive.

NEGOTIATING AN OFFER

Usually a potential purchaser starts any discussion about an offer by asking the agent 'what do you think Mr Vendor will accept?' To this the agent has to reply that he does not know, but 'please make an offer which is sensible and be prepared to discuss it.' The purchaser will then name a figure which the agent may or may not discuss with him.

- The agent has a legal duty to tell you about all offers received regardless of the amount of the offer.

- Unless specifically instructed in writing your agent may not accept or refuse an offer without your instructions.

- The law also requires all agents to confirm all offers in writing in the next day's post.

You must be given the opportunity to decide on the course of action to be taken. Detailed notes with time and date should be kept following each conversation with the purchaser and your agent. These can be most helpful to clarify points in later discussions or if a dispute arises.

Opening negotiations

The monetary figure is only part of the make-up of an offer. In considering whether to accept you will need to know whether finance is available, whether the offer depends on the sale of another property and if so whether a buyer has been found. You will seek reassurance that the purchaser is genuine and will not frivolously back out after putting you to a lot of trouble and expense on wasted legal fees.

Your agent will ask pertinent questions concerning the background to the offer and where possible check the truth of statements made by your potential purchaser. In their eagerness to drive a bargain some purchasers resort to lies about their financial status which only becomes clear later.

Negotiating notes

Sunday 9th May

Mr and Mrs Brown viewed.

Wednesday 12th May
2pm Wife received telephone call from our agent to say that Mr Purchaser was offering £30,000 (our asking price is £39,500). Wife told the agent that she will discuss it with me on my return from the cash & carry. She asked the agent to confirm that Mr Brown had enough money in cash as he gave the impression that he needed to borrow a substantial proportion.

3pm. I phoned the agent refusing the offer.

4pm. Agent phoned to say that he had checked with Mr Brown that he had sufficient funds and had raised his offer to £33,000. Replied that I would give my reply in the morning as we were at the moment very busy and needed to talk about it. Agent's view that this was a good offer from a serious buyer who was able to proceed.

Thursday 13th May
10am. Told agent we would accept £36,500.

10.30 Agent phoned to say that Mr Brown's final offer was £35,000. I said I would need to discuss it with my accountant but I was not inclined to accept.

10.45 Agent again phoned to say he had told Mr Brown my position and Mr Brown said that he would pay £36,500 if I included the trailer. We accepted.

Fig. 22. Example of negotiating notes.

An offer for a lock-up business from a person with the full purchase price held in a building society and living locally is very different from an offer of the same amount (or even more) from a person living elsewhere who after the sale of his house will still require to borrow 50% of the purchase price. The former offer is better because he is in a position to purchase without delay. The latter has to arrange finance, sell or let his house, move and find accommodation locally before the sale can be completed. The permutations are endless and each offer has to be viewed on its merits.

Responding to the offer

You have to decide whether to refuse, accept or make a counter offer. In all negotiations it is very wise to remain truthful because all statements must be capable of substantiation if challenged.

Although it may be tempting, it is illegal and dishonest to invent alternative purchasers in order to push up an offer. In practice this usually ends in failure. If there really is a second purchaser in the offing then this fact can be used in the negotiations. When a sale is proceeding it can be risky to introduce a second purchaser, who may be offering a higher price as a way of raising the first purchaser. Should another person express a wish to buy your business then it is wiser to keep the second purchaser on hold in case the first falls through, rather than swap purchasers for no better reason than price. If the first person is in difficulty then of course the swap can be taken seriously.

Do's and dont's of negotiation

1. During any negotiations it is vital never to tell a lie, and never to get into a position from which you cannot move because that will be the end of the negotiation. Anything which is said has to be firm and yet provide room for discussion until both parties genuinely reach the point from which they will not move. Quiet tact and polite diplomacy achieve the best results. Too much discussion and contact during negotiations can be as detrimental as too little and it is a matter of subtle judgment as to when and how to initiate each contact.

2. It is during price negotiations that your agent usually proves invaluable. By going through him, time is given for the principals to consider their position carefully before each response. It gives time for each side to reassess their finances, look at alternatives, negotiate over fixtures, fittings and equipment as well as the contract price. It gives time for tempers to cool.

3. Although there is no compulsion to use your agent in the negotiating process it usually ensures a better outcome. The agent is experienced in negotiating and can often make helpful suggestions which will satisfy both parties. He has experience in how much to say, how to persuade and how to confirm a deal. He is much less emotionally involved than you are and so can see things more objectively and calmly. He has a duty to obtain the best price for you, his client, and a good agent will bear this in mind throughout all discussions.

4. With some negotiations immediate reactions to offers and counter offers are best. With others a pause before answering can prove the best way of proceeding.

5. At each point, be clear about the exact terms you are being offered or are offering the other party. Sometimes a general discussion about price is understood as an offer by one party but not by the other. Sometimes misunderstandings occur about what is or is not included in the offer. Special terms such as the extent of any training, the time scale for acceptance of the offer, time limit for completion and so on must be spelt out unequivocally.

6. The offer package may include or exclude furnishings, tools, ancillary equipment, vehicles, who is paying the landlord's legal fees and so on. As soon as a verbal agreement has been reached it must be put in writing with copies to each party and this is normally done by your agent. Such statements are not contracts for sale but do prevent some highly charged misunderstandings surfacing at a later date.

Every negotiation is different and experience can be dearly bought. You will be in a strong position if there is little pressure on you to sell and in a weak position if there is a lot of pressure on you to sell through ill health or finance, for example. Whatever the situation, a realistic approach to market forces will dictate your final agreement.

On-going negotiating

Unfortunately the initial agreement of the price with a purchaser may not be the end of the negotiations. Price discussions can arise after a property or specialist financial survey, after the purchaser's solicitor has viewed the terms of the lease or lease/purchase agreements, after the purchaser finds he may have insufficient financial resources to meet the original agreed price, and so on. The primary negotiations may well have been conducted in good faith but they are not legally binding.

There are different circumstances for sales in Scotland and sales by auction, so if either of these apply then you must take appropriate advice before offering your business for sale.

The nervous tensions surrounding negotiations cannot be totally removed until the sale is complete and the money received. Additional negotiations and agreements will be required over stock levels and valuation procedures, handover dates, and treatment of customers with outstanding bills. Some of the discussions you may not think of as 'negotiations' as they will appear quite normal sensible arrangements to

Example of letter of agreement

Dear Mr Peter Purchaser,

Re: XYZ Stores, London Road

I am writing to confirm our various telephone conversations and your offer to purchase my above business and leasehold property for the sum of £36,500 leasehold, subject to contract. Stock to be purchased separately at valuation. The trailer and all fixtures and fittings as listed on our sales details are included. The costs of the landlord's legal fees to be shared equally between us.

You told me that you have cash available to purchase the business and will only require a loan to buy the stock and you have an appointment at your bank next Wednesday.

Can you please let me have a note confirming that you will proceed with the purchase immediately, subject to contract, and finance for the purchase of the stock.

At the same time can you tell me the name and address of your solicitor, name and address of your bank and the details of two referees. There is no need for you to approach the referees because my solicitor will be writing. The references are required by the landlord for the transfer of the lease to you.

My solicitor is Mr ..... of the Town Partnership, 10 Smith Street, ... and I have told him about our deal.

I hope you will be very happy and successful with the shop and assure you that we shall do everything we can to ensure a smooth handover.

Yours sincerely

John Vendor
Copy to: Mr ....., Town Partnership, Solicitors.

Fig. 23. Example of letter of agreement.

make under the circumstances.

Where there is a spirit of co-operation these subsidiary negotiations go along smoothly and almost unnoticed. However where this friendly co-operation turns to acrimony they can test the strongest nerves and easily lead to a calling off of the sale by either party. Hence the reasons to have the major terms of your sale properly recorded when goodwill is at its optimum level.

Following through your agreement

Except in Scotland and in auctions, sales are agreed **subject to contract**. This means that any or all terms of the sale can be altered by mutual agreement up to the moment the contracts for the sale are exchanged. This is usually between one and three months after you have come to your initial agreement. The purchaser's solicitor has the opportunity to examine and satisfy himself on behalf of his client about the ownership of the business and property and the terms of any leases, finance agreements, maintenance contracts, guarantees and so on before his client is irrevocably committed to the purchase.

While the contract is being drawn up the purchaser may also have the property surveyed to learn of any building defects and needy repairs. He can also have his accountant look at the trading accounts in detail. At any time before the exchange of contracts you or the purchaser can withdraw from the sale without any further obligations and the costs incurred have to be carried by each party. The exception is when the purchaser agrees to pay a deposit at the outset and agrees that if he withdraws your expenses can be deducted from the deposit. It is fairly unusual for purchasers to agree to this but there is no harm in suggesting such a condition during the price negotiation.

SUMMARY

We have considered the arrangements for showing potential purchasers round the business and property and reaching a clear agreement. The need for patience, calmness and integrity has been demonstrated to achieve a sale without loss of dignity. We have then discussed ways of protecting the terms of the sale and the useful role played by a good agent. In the next chapter we will discuss the process leading up to exchange of contracts.

CASE STUDIES

Chris and Joan get ready for viewings
The price suggested by the agent is well below the figure Chris has

quoted in the local advertisement. Chris decides to quote a figure to any replies from the trade journal advertisement halfway between his own assessment and the business transfer agent's figure. There are eleven replies. Eight ask the price, three of whom will not give their names but keep on asking questions about the business. One is an agent seeking instructions and the other two leave Chris wondering why they called at all. The final outcome is for two couples to view. Appointments are made but only one party turns up. Nothing further is heard from the other.

The viewers spend two hours looking and appear very critical of every detail. Everything is wrong. At the end they said 'with an effort we could do something with this place,' and offer a figure well below even the agent's figure. All Chris' pent up worry boils over in an angry outburst and he tells the viewers to leave immediately even though they are in the middle of a cup of tea.

Afterwards Chris and Joan have one of their rare arguments. Chris feels humiliated and Joan feels guilty because her normal hospitality has been violated. Finally they agree to call the agent and ask his advice about the offer. The agent offers to negotiate with their viewer and quotes a fee to be paid if successful. Chris accepts and awaits the result impatiently.

Mabel: the good news and the bad news
Mabel is suddenly stimulated by an offer from her original enquirer. She thinks it is a good one and tells her agent about it, hoping to save herself and the agent money. The agent agrees to handle all aspects of the sale for half his normal fee. On making enquiries of the proposed purchaser the agent discovers that he has a property to sell and even when sold he is unlikely to have sufficient funds. He bluntly tells this to the purchaser. Mabel then starts to overhear remarks in the village as to how greedy she is about the price she is asking. She traces the source to the discomfited purchaser and faces him.

A further three months passes with only two viewers. They are not interested because they see how much work has to be done on the property. Just as Mabel is wondering whether to go on with the sole agency agreement or appoint another agent she has a viewer who makes an offer only a little below the asking price. She accepts. A survey finds a number of problems of which only one is really serious and the price is renegotiated through the agent.

Brian's and Jill's weekend rush
Six sets of viewers come to see the kennels. When fixing the day Brian and Jill have forgotten that this weekend is likely to be the busiest of

the year. It is towards the end of the school holidays and customers are arriving to deposit and collect their dogs. Brian and Jill try to remember what each party of viewers have said. By Monday they are exhausted and realise too late they should have written down the salient points. They know one party wants some turnover figures and another party is more interested in the number of customers and where they come from – but neither Brian nor Jill remember who has asked for what. They do their best and hope they get it right. Brian and Jill also become aware that they are slipping back into rows and work hard to control themselves.

A week later they have a phone call with an offer from a group whom they hardly noticed in the rush. It is a figure they feel they can just accept but then Brian curtly refuses it and feels unable to discuss it further. While Brian is out next day Jill phones the people up and explains that Brian is not feeling well – will they consider splitting the difference? The purchasers agree to phone back later. Brian answers the phone and cannot understand at first why the purchasers speak about Jill's suggestion and ask 'if he is feeling better'. Brian realises what Jill has done and is furious. He controls himself sufficiently to be polite and agree the new figure. The purchasers then go on to ask if Brian and Jill can be out by the end of the month as they have all the money for the purchase held in a building society and are at present living in a rented house.

POINTS FOR DISCUSSION

1. What other ways are there of reacting to offers and what questions would you ask the purchaser about his offer?

2. What steps can you take to give yourself time to talk to viewers?

3. In what ways could you persuade a purchaser to increase a low offer into an acceptable figure?

Handling viewings and negotations

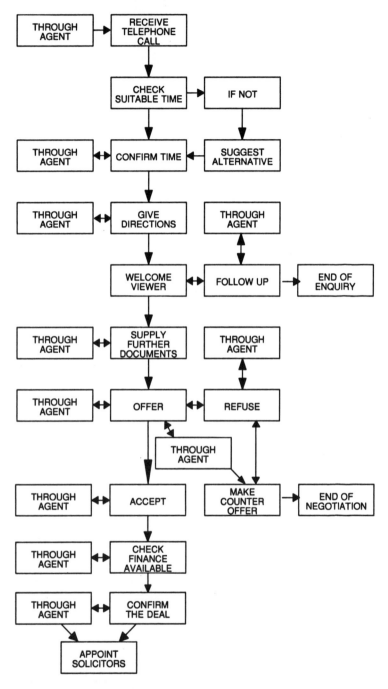

Fig. 24. The viewing and negotiating process.

6
From Offer to
Exchange of Contracts

WHAT THIS CHAPTER WILL TELL YOU

The stage has been reached when you and your purchaser have agreed
a price and terms for a deal. These terms then become subject to a
formal contract usually prepared and agreed by solicitors before it
becomes binding. As mentioned in the previous chapter, sales in
Scotland and by auction undergo a different legal process which is
not dealt with here. Any solicitor can give the relevant information.
Nevertheless, many of the practical points will apply to a business
being sold in Scotland.

SORTING OUT THE PROCESS

The legal process for selling differs between businesses. Some have
leasehold property, others freehold property, and those which have
neither. The process differs between businesses which are incorporated as limited companies and those which are sole traders or
partnerships. Some businesses owe their existence to a **franchise** or
licence agreement. Yet others offered for sale are a part of a much
larger business, eg a branch shop of a retail chain.

When considering the sale of your business one or more of the
following paragraphs may apply and the deal can become quite
complex. For example, you may be offering a fast food franchise
outlet for sale. Your franchise is owned by your limited company and
the limited company leases the premises from you. In these
circumstances the purchaser buys the shares of your limited company
to secure the franchise and in a separate contract the limited company
buys the freehold from you. As the ownership of the limited company
is changing your purchaser will also have to satisfy the franchisor as
well, although the franchise is vested in the limited company. In a sale
like this you and your purchaser will be guided through by the

solicitors and accountants.

Choosing a solicitor

Most business sales involve a solicitor and selecting one can seem a major obstacle. All solicitors owe a clear duty to their clients, and will perform this duty in a more or less compatible way. Your agent or a friend may make a recommendation.

Solicitors' fees can vary considerably from one firm to another. Do enquire about likely costs and obtain written quotations. If you have not already met then you should at least see the solicitor before giving any instructions to proceed. You should feel comfortable with your advisers and confident in their ability to look after your interests. It is best to sort this out and brief the solicitor before the need arises so that the solicitor can have the background documents ready on file.

Selling a franchise

You should be able to offer all prospective purchasers a copy of

- the current franchise agreement

- the company prospectus, and

- sales literature

The agreement offered to your purchaser may differ in some respects from your own as changes in the franchise may have been introduced to which you are not party. Such changes may enhance or lower the value of your franchise. For your own reasons, you may want to delay telling your franchisor about your plans to sell but whatever you decide you should remain within the written conditions of your own agreement.

Many purchasers will want the franchise document checked by their own solicitor who may suggest amendments. Any such changes would have to be negotiated with and accepted by the franchisor. You would have no part in these discussions and can only await the outcome although your purchaser may ask you about any practical outworkings of the franchise. Where there is property then a normal business property sale will also be involved.

Usually the **conveyance** and the **application for the franchise** can run concurrently, though some purchasers prefer to sort out the one before embarking on the other.

Selling a private limited company

During the negotiation your purchaser will have agreed to buy the shares in the limited company which runs the business.

- For sales which include leasehold or freehold property there will be solicitors involved, primarily to check the title and related property information. There will also be accountants to work through and agree the financial detail.

- For businesses which do not include property the sale may be dealt with by accountants alone.

Since there are so many parties working on the transaction, communication between them becomes all important. Both the agent and the principals need to ensure that the work is getting done, correspondence dealt with and misunderstandings avoided. Everybody who has been caught up in business sales can quote examples of how all parties have been quietly sitting back waiting for each other to act. Only when they are stirred is there any action.

A limited company without property
When all parties involved are familiar with the business and a price has been agreed this can change ownership very quickly by the transfer of the shares. An accountant will be needed to oversee the completion of statutory requirements under the various Companies Acts, effect the necessary registrations and to draw up a balance sheet.

SELLING A BUSINESS WITHOUT PROPERTY

In these business sales, solicitors or other legal representatives may not be necessary. Businesses where no property is involved include for example newsrounds, van selling, home based concerns, and domestic repair services.

The sales of these businesses are often completed within a week or two of the first meeting. Home-based franchised businesses involve little more than the above plus the agreement of the franchisor.

Although the use of a solicitor is not mandatory, either party may be unsure of the procedures or of their rights. You may have serious concerns and decide to talk the sale through with your usual legal adviser. Although a verbal agreement can be proof of a legal contract for sale, particularly if money changes hands, it is good sense for you and your purchaser to put an outline of your agreement in writing. It is amazing how often failure to take this simple precaution leads to trouble later. The document does not have to be complicated by legal jargon as long as the intention is clear and expressed in simple language. It should be in duplicate with copies signed and kept by each party. It does not matter who makes the draft, but if you do so you will keep the initiative.

Drafting a letter of agreement
The title of the business, special terms, inclusions and exclusions, must be stated. There must be sufficient information to define the business identity and what is to be included in the sale. This may appear obvious but it is surprising how often it is omitted on the assumption that 'of course everyone knows what the document is all about.'

The document may need careful wording, particularly if you are selling only part of your business. For example, you may own a garage and operate a vehicle home-tune business which you have decided to sell as a separate entity. The agreement will need to specify unequivocally the limit of operation of your garage, as well as that of the home tune business and the separate names of each business.

When you start to write out the agreement you may find it more complex than you first thought and call for help with the wording from your agent, solicitor or accountant.

- **Stating what is included for the money**. In most cases this appears clear when the deal is struck, but misunderstandings can and do occur. The agreement needs to list what equipment, vehicles, stationery and so on is being sold; what training you are going to give; and how you will introduce your purchaser to customers and suppliers.

- **Making handover arrangements**. This concerns how, when and where the payment for the business will be made. You can safeguard receipt of the money by specifying that payment be made by bankers' draft, a building society cheque, or by cash. It could even be held by an independent third party. If your purchaser objects to paying by one of these relatively secure methods, you may question his financial probity and be even more cautious.

- **Safeguarding the purchaser's interest**. Your purchaser may ask you to give an undertaking not to set up in competition to the business you are selling for a period of time (usually two years) within the geographical area in which the business operates. The distance will depend on the nature of the business.

```
┌─────────────────────────────────────────────────────────┐
│              Checking the sales agreement                │
│                                                          │
│                                             Checklist    │
│  Have you stated who the agreement is between?   Yes/No   │
│                                                          │
│  Have you identified the business?               Yes/No   │
│                                                          │
│  Have you stated the price?                      Yes/No   │
│                                                          │
│  Have you stated what equipment is included?     Yes/No   │
│                                                          │
│  Have you specified the training period?         Yes/No   │
│                                                          │
│  Have you said how the introductions are going to be     │
│      done?                                       Yes/No   │
│                                                          │
│  Have you agreed how to deal with outstanding            │
│      accounts?                                   Yes/No   │
│                                                          │
│  Have you stated how the stock is to be valued?  Yes/No   │
│                                                          │
│  Have you said how you will be paid for the business? Yes/No │
│                                                          │
│  Have you given an undertaking not to compete?   Yes/No   │
│                                                          │
│  Have you stated when and where handover takes           │
│      place?                                      Yes/No   │
└─────────────────────────────────────────────────────────┘
```

Fig. 25. Points to cover in your sale agreement.

SELLING A BUSINESS WITH FREEHOLD PROPERTY

The conveyance of a business with freehold property involves the same legal process as a normal freehold domestic residence, with the addition of the terms and conditions relating to the business.

The contract for sale will include clauses covering

- stock valuation and payment
- equipment on lease/purchase
- safeguards to the purchaser of the business
- licences
- trading permissions
- shop fixtures and fittings
- office equipment
- manufacturing and repair tools
- intellectual rights
- training arrangements
- staff terms, and
- a breakdown of the sale price into a freehold property value, a fixtures and fittings value and a goodwill value.

Agreement letter

24th June 1994

Dear Mr and Mrs Purchaser

Following our conversations I agree to sell you my newspaper rounds in the .... area and the goodwill attaching thereto for the sum of £17,500, including the computer hardware and associated programmes. The handover will take place on Sunday 4th July 1994 in exchange for certified cheques drawn in my favour.

I undertake to be available for a minimum of 2 weeks from Monday 28th June 1994 to introduce you to the customers, the rounds and my method of running the business. Prior to handing over I shall introduce you to the wholesalers. The training to include a minimum of 2 evenings instruction on the computer and computer system. If any longer period for handover should be required this will be arranged by mutual agreement. I have no intention of selling newspapers in the area again and formally undertake not to do so within five miles of .... for a period of three years from the date of the sale of the business to you.

I agree to collect as much as possible of outstanding monies from customers before handover. You agree to purchase from me any unpaid customer accounts and I shall reimburse you for any monies still outstanding more than three months after you take over. I shall settle with all suppliers in full for any goods delivered prior to handover.

I shall consider this agreement as binding on us both on return of a copy signed by you.

Yours sincerely,

John Vendor

Agreed ....

(Mr Purchaser/Mrs Purchaser), (date)

Witness ....
Address ....
....
....
....

Fig 26. Sample letter of agreement drawn up between you and your purchaser.

Confirming the sale to your solicitor

I have agreed to sell my business and property to Mr Purchaser
for the sum of £.......... Full details are being sent to you by
XYZ agent of .... The deeds are held by ABC building society
at .... and you have my authority to have them released to
your charge.

We hope to complete as soon as possible.

Fig. 27. Sample of letter to your solicitor confirming the sale.

Agent's letter

Dear Mr and Mrs Vendor,

Ref: G123 – Post Office Stores, Smith Road

We refer to the various telephone discussions and
correspondence over the last few weeks and write to confirm your
proposed sale of the above business and freehold property to Mr
Purchaser of [address] for the sum of £[   ] freehold, subject to
contract. Stock to be sold separately at valuation.
We have written to your solicitors, Messrs. J. Solicitors & Co,
giving the relevant details, as per copy letter attached.
Can you please confirm in writing your acceptance of this offer
to sell your business and freehold property, subject to contract,
and also forward to us a list of the fixtures and fittings you have
agreed to include in the transaction.
We trust that this matter will now go forward to a speedy and
satisfactory completion. We have been assured that Mr Purchaser
has agreed a loan in principle with his bank and therefore is in a
position to proceed.
Please contact us if you have any queries.

Yours sincerely,

A. B. Business Transfer Agents.

Fig. 28. Sample of letter from your agent confirming the sale.

Sample of letter from a business transfer agent to your solicitor

Messrs J. Solicitors & Co
Solicitors

For the Attention of Mr Lawyer

Dear Sirs,

Your clients: Mr and Mrs Vendor
Re XY Post Office Stores, Smith Road
Our Ref: G123

We write to confirm that your clients Mr and Mrs Vendor of XY Post Office Stores, Smith Road have agreed to sell the above business and freehold property, for the sum of £[   ], subject to contract and the purchaser being appointed sub-postmaster. Stock to be sold separately at valuation.

The proposed buyer is Mr Purchaser of [   ] and the solicitors acting on his behalf are Messrs Legal Beavers of [   ] – attention Mr Barrister.

A copy of the sales details is enclosed and we have asked for a list of the fixtures and fittings. On receipt we shall forward a copy.

Both parties have indicated that they would like to exchange contracts as quickly as possible with completion on 30th June 1994. We understand that Mr Purchaser has had the approval of the necessary finance in principle from his bank and he is contacting the Post Office for the sub postmaster application forms.

We trust the foregoing is satisfactory for your purposes and if we can be of any further assistance, please do not hesitate to contact us.

Yours faithfully,

A. B. Business Transfer Agents

copy to Mr Vendor (for information)

Fig. 29. Sample of letter from a business transfer agent to your solicitor.

Fig. 30. Sample reply to your agent.

Looking at a surveyor's report

If your purchaser needs a loan the building society or bank will insist
on their having a **property survey** and **valuation**. Unfortunately many
purchasers are quite unprepared for the detailed comments listed on a
typical surveyor's report. They may withdraw from the purchase
immediately, try to renegotiate the price, seek reassurance that the
property is not about to fall down, or ask for an undertaking that the
specific repairs are carried out before completion.

   You will feel relieved after the survey report has been read and
accepted by your purchaser and his bank or building society.

Requests for a business survey

A bank may also ask for a survey from a specialist agency before
offering a loan. Either or both these surveys may be completed before
the solicitors are instructed to prepare draft contracts or whilst this
work is proceeding. You may not wish to incur solicitor's and
accountant's charges until survey reports have been read and
accepted, but this will depend on your own circumstances.

Instructing your solicitor

When a business transfer agent has introduced your purchaser then
your agent will gather in and provide the information needed by the

solicitors. Your solicitor will seek confirmation from you and not start work without it. You can send him a straightforward letter (see figure 27).

Telling your solicitor what he needs to know

If an agent is not involved then you will need to tell your solicitor:

- The price agreed.

- The name and address of your purchaser and the firm of solicitors acting for him.

- Any special terms and conditions agreed during the negotiations.

- The date you are seeking to complete the sale and hand over the business.

- The breakdown of the agreed price between the freehold property, the fixtures and fittings and the goodwill. These figures are not essential at the initial stage of the conveyance but do discuss and agree them with your accountant as soon as possible. There are likely to be tax implications which need to be considered.

Giving your solicitor the documents he needs

Your solicitor will need to have the following:

The property deeds or lease
Many property deeds and original leases are held by building societies, banks or insurance companies. Your solicitor will probably require your authorisation for them to be released to his charge.

The documents appertaining to any licences
lease/purchase agreements, loans, planning permissions, building repair guarantees and so on.

A list of the fixtures, fittings and equipment
included in the purchase. This list should include all major items in the business and in the living accommodation. Anything which is subject to a leasing or lease/purchase agreement will need to be mentioned.

A list of any items you have agreed to sell separately
to your purchaser.

During the legal process the solicitor acting for the purchaser will raise a series of detailed questions which you must answer to the best of your knowledge. Additional documents may be called for.

Telling your advisers
You need to tell your bank and/or building society about your proposed sale so that your solicitor can apply for the precise total of repayments which have to be paid out of the proceeds of the sale. Your accountant needs to know so that final accounts can be prepared quickly.

SELLING A BUSINESS WITH LEASEHOLD PROPERTY

The conveyance of a business with leasehold property is similar with the addition of the **assignment of the lease** to your purchaser.

Your solicitor will need the original lease and other documents as listed above.

Obtaining purchaser references
A bank and two other references will be needed by your landlord and these will be obtained either by your solicitor or your agent. As long as the references are satisfactory the landlord cannot normally withhold his approval of the purchaser, although he may ask to meet him. The landlord's solicitor has to prepare a **licence to assign** without undue delay after receiving the references and referring them to your landlord for his approval.

Paying the landlord's solicitor
The solicitor acting for the landlord may seek a guarantee that his fee will be paid before taking any action. There is no rule as to who should pay the fees. However the purchaser generally pays the fee where a commercial property changes hands, and the vendor where retail premises are involved. Sometimes the cost is shared because it can be argued that ultimately both benefit from the transaction. To complicate the matter further the practice varies from one part of the country to another and with each person's previous experiences.

Regrettably these costs often become a bone of contention, and so the question should be thrashed out at the time of the original offer to purchase. It can be a useful tool during the price negotiation.

Dealing with a survey
As with a freehold property your purchaser may decide to have a **structural survey**. The condition of the property will be compared with

the requirements of the lease. The report can sometimes identify repairs and decorations, in the form of a **schedule of dilapidations** and you will have to agree with your purchaser whether to make an adjustment on the price or complete the work yourself. Broadly speaking, the landlord will expect the property to be maintained. At the end of the lease he can demand that repairs are carried out by the lessee to the standard laid down in the lease.

MOVING TOWARDS EXCHANGE OF CONTRACTS

Asking for a deposit

You may feel more at ease if your purchaser pays a **returnable deposit** to be held by your agent, solicitor or accountant. Such deposits only have the value of making both parties feel more committed to the transaction. Your purchaser may feel more confident that you will not back out or sell to another party if he has given a deposit and you may feel more certain that your purchaser will go through with the agreement and not back off lightly.

Many business transfer agents and solicitors no longer suggest asking for deposits because for them they have very little meaning. Experience tells them that purchasers have no hesitation in asking for the return of the deposit. As pointed out in the previous chapter, non-returnable deposits which can be used to reimburse legal fees are sometimes negotiated as a condition of sale. Such conditions are generally unpopular with purchasers and the practice of holding deposits is gradually dying out. The exception is the non-returnable deposit which is handed over to your solicitor on exchange of contracts. Even here there are changes, because until quite recently this was always 10% of the purchase price; now it is any reasonable amount which can be offered by the purchaser.

Living through the period between the offer and the exchange

Once the initial negotiations have been completed, enquiries made as to the finance, and solicitors instructed, there is usually a period of unnatural calm. During this period you have a duty to your purchaser to run the business in the normal way. It is a period of strain for vendor and purchaser alike, and great care is needed to avoid misunderstandings. Your purchaser will be eager to allay his own anxieties by wanting more information about your business; you may be reluctant to pass on the information until you are utterly convinced that the purchaser will complete.

Although the purchaser may press you to make changes in anticipation of completion you should resist until after exchange of contracts. To give an extreme example, one purchaser asked that all stock be sold before completion, but at the very last moment – when exchange and completion had been arranged to take place on the same day – he backed off and the vendor found he had no business. The vendor was left with worthless empty leasehold premises, his own and the landlord's legal expenses and a bitter experience.

Working together before exchange
You may be faced with a request from the purchaser to work beside you while the solicitors are preparing the contract. In most instances it is wiser to avoid this.

- First, because both parties already have a high level of anxiety, and the smallest disagreement can provoke a major argument.

- Secondly there is no protection from the purchaser learning how to run the business during this period and then setting up in competition.

- Thirdly you may have all you can cope with in planning and preparing for your own move and running the business efficiently, without having to begin training the purchaser.

- Fourthly by having the purchaser with you there is no way of keeping news of the sale away from staff and customers.

There may well be an advantage for both parties if the practical training is agreed to take place only after the exchange of contracts and before the completion date.

Keeping the relationship businesslike
The best sales are achieved when you and your purchaser keep a friendly, businesslike approach to each other throughout. Differences are best resolved either through your agent or the solicitors. Neither of these parties are emotionally involved and any delay brought about by dealing through third parties allows time for tempers to cool and also time for careful more balanced thought.

Communicating between agent, solicitors and their clients
If you try to telephone the solicitor acting for your purchaser to get some action, that solicitor will quite properly refuse to respond and explain that he can only respond to requests received from his client or through your solicitor. Your agent however can quite properly

Getting up to date – checklist

	Circle
Have you written up all your accounts?	Yes/No
Have you removed all unsaleable stock?	Yes/No
Have you thrown out all unwanted possessions?	Yes/No
Have you done any building repairs which you promised?	Yes/No
Have you done any machine repairs which you promised?	Yes/No
Have you selected your stock valuer?	Yes/No
Have you selected your furniture removers?	Yes/No
Have you the forms for asking for the meters to be read?	Yes/No
Have you drafted letters to customers?	Yes/No
Have you drafted letters to suppliers?	Yes/No
Have you prepared a notice?	Yes/No
Have you prepared change of address cards for friends?	Yes/No
Have you prepared change of address cards for relatives?	Yes/No
Have you prepared helpful instructions for your purchaser?	Yes/No
Have you prepared a list of suppliers for your purchaser?	Yes/No
Have you prepared a list of customers for your purchaser?	Yes/No
Have you listed what needs to be done after exchange?	Yes/No
Have you listed what needs to be done on handover day?	Yes/No
Have you planned whom to ask to help you move?	Yes/No
Have you arranged for insurance on your new home?	Yes/No
Have you planned what to do with the money?	Yes/No
Have you thought what else you can do in advance?	Yes/No

Fig. 31. Getting your affairs up-to-date.

approach all parties direct. He is in the best position to resolve differences and to find out the causes of any unaccountable delays. The agent can report the reasons to the purchaser, or yourself, and propose a course of action.

Dealing with anxieties
Regular information about the progress of the conveyance can do much to help everyone through this difficult period. The solicitors and the agent share this responsibility. During this time, you too may be buying a home and fulfilling the role of purchaser as well. Thus you may be in a dual role of seller and buyer, carrying a double anxiety which makes you feel vulnerable and insecure.

Getting up to date
You may be able to subdue some anxieties by throwing yourself into odd jobs which have been put off but now have to be done, for example, bringing the bookkeeping entries up to date, throwing out old unsaleable stock, chucking away unwanted possessions, preparing letters to suppliers and change of address notices, obtaining quotations for removal and stock valuation, readying application forms for the meter readings and telephone transfer, and so on.

There are many such tasks which have to be finished before the sale. Lists of arrangements can be made, with dates. None of these activities affect other people, nor are they likely to breach confidentiality but all preparations which can be made in advance will be of considerable benefit later when contracts have been exchanged.

From the outset one party or the other has an idea of the best time for handover, and solicitors are often given a target date. For some legal and taxation purposes the important relevant date is the exchange of contracts, rather than completion, and if there is any doubt you should check with your accountant. For example, is your tax liability affected if you exchange before or after the end of the tax year on 5th April?

The signal that this period of limbo is ending is when you are asked to visit your solicitor to sign the contract and agree a date for completion. Frequently there is a misconception that the act of signing the contract document by both parties binds them to the deal. This is not so; the contract becomes binding only from the moment they are exchanged (usually between solicitors). The telephone call from your solicitor telling you that the exchange has been effected is when the first bottle of champagne may be broached. The second bottle may be broached when you have the money from the sale.

HANDING OVER THE STOCK

Allaying suspicions

The amount of stock held by a business varies so much from day to day that sale of the stock for a predetermined sum can lead to gross unfairness to one party or the other. It can also lead to the suspicion of a deliberate distortion.

'Stock at valuation'

As a general rule, when there is a stock of goods, raw materials or partly manufactured items being passed over, the purchaser agrees in the contract to buy them **at valuation**. You may have agreed a maximum value because this is the total which your purchaser can afford; or you may have agreed to exclude certain classes of goods; you may have agreed to accept payment by instalment. Whatever the arrangement a valuation must be made of the stock being handed over with the business.

Dealing with the VAT

When a business is sold the stock is transferred net of VAT when both parties are registered for VAT or an application for registration has been made. If in doubt you should refer to your local enquiry office of the Customs and Excise.

Valuing the stock

There are three basic approaches.

1. Valuing by you and your purchaser.

This involves you and your purchaser going through the stock together and agreeing the values. This approach is most used when only a small amount of stock, or only a few items of large value are involved and invoices are available. When a larger or more diffuse stock is involved, differences of opinion can arise on cost values, particularly for older stock, or on saleability. This is a distressing experience for both parties and will sour an otherwise smooth sale. The solicitors may advise putting a clause in the contract detailing a procedure when there is a stock valuation dispute which cannot be resolved amicably.

Usually you and your purchasers have much else to do on the day of handover because there is so much information to be passed concerning customers, suppliers, the property and the way various items of equipment are operated. You may decide to sidestep several hours spent valuing stock, with the very real risk for bitter argument,

Stock valuation by Vendor and Purchaser

Stock Valuation Certificate
Business/Premises_____

We confirm that the total stock of the above business has been valued by us jointly and we unreservedly accept as fair and correct the valuation figures below. We accept that:

1. The valuation only applies on the date of the valuation and neither party can subsequently enter into any dispute on the valuation figures.

2. The valuation is based on cost values (using agreed profit margins where appropriate) or assessed realisable values if lower.

3. The valuation covers only those goods allowed for in the contract of sale and owned and paid for by the vendor of the business.

Stock item	*Valuation*
VAT standard rated goods	£_____
VAT zero rated goods	£_____
Accounts receivable transferred	£_____
Business consumables	£_____
TOTAL VALUE EXCLUSIVE OF VAT	£_____

Fig. 32. Example of a stock valuation certificate when the valuation is carried out by the vendor and purchaser. You will each need a signed copy for your accountants.

and appoint **stock valuers** instead. They will then decide on values and saleability of all items.

2. Using stock valuers and sharing the expense
The most usual method is for independent reputable stock valuers to be appointed to act jointly for you and your purchaser. You will probably be asked to be present at the beginning and at the end of the valuation and you will have the right to observe while the work is being done if you wish. The valuers' fee – which is usually based on a percentage (with a minimum) of the net value of the stock – can be shared equally between you.

The valuers may work direct from cost prices gleaned from invoices supplied or from their own cost information or they may work from retail prices and deduct average gross profit margins which have been agreed by all parties. They may work from a mixture of both methods as it largely depends on the nature of the stock they are valuing. In manufacturing they will work on a value added basis.

The valuers will work on the day of handover whether it is a weekday or weekend and with the least disturbance of the stock. They will continue until they finish whatever the time of day or night.

As soon as they finish the valuers will compute the total cost value of the stock and/or work in progress so that payment can be made at once and the keys handed over.

3. Valuing the stock and not sharing the cost
You and your purchaser may each decide to appoint your own stock valuers. This happens most frequently when a chain of retail shops buys or sells a retail unit, as many companies will only use their own valuers. A purchaser or vendor may either accept their valuation or appoint their own stock valuers to protect their own interests. Each firm of stock valuers makes its own assessment of the stock value and at the end compares totals and reaches agreement. You and your purchaser are then told the total and payment is made in the usual way. Using two firms of stock valuers is more costly because both teams will need to be paid in full by their principals instead of the cost of one team of valuers being shared between you and your purchaser.

Valuing stock – other points to consider
Apart from physical goods, other items can be included as stock. For example, goods supplied to customers on credit terms, or outstanding newspaper accounts. Within the terms of the contract for sale there will be a clause safeguarding the purchaser if payments for goods or services which you have supplied and included in the stock handover

STOCK VALUATION CERTIFICATE

Business/Premises_____

We confirm that the total stock of the above business has been valued by representatives of A. B. Valuers Ltd and we unreservedly accept as fair and correct the valuation figures below. We accept that:

- The valuation only applies on the date of the valuation and A.B. Valuers cannot subsequently enter into any dispute on the valuation figures.

- Unless any categories for special treatment have been agreed by all parties beforehand the valuation is based on cost values or using agreed profit margins where appropriate or assessed realisable values if lower.

- It is not the responsibility of A. B. Valuers to verify ownership of merchandise.

Item	Valuation
VAT standard rated goods	£_____
VAT zero rated goods	£_____
Accounts receivable transferred	£_____
Business consumables	£_____
TOTAL VALUE EXCLUSIVE OF VAT	£_____

Vendor_____ Purchaser_____

Date of valuation_____ Valuer_____

Fig. 33. Example of stock valuer's certificate.

value, are not received. Any goods which have been prepaid are discounted or ignored as are any lines held on a sale of return basis.

There are a few business sales where the stock is included in the overall price of the business because its value is only a fraction of the agreed price. Examples can be taken from the service industry when there is unused copy paper, envelopes, general stationery and so on.

There are other business sales where there is no stock to be sold on. The sale may be of empty business premises where your purchaser will be starting a new business venture and you have agreed to sell off the stock.

For yet others the stock is renewed daily or at the end of each week and both parties agree that no stock will be taken over by the purchaser. This could apply to cafés, greengrocers and other shops selling only fresh produce, or to a business which is changing supplier, for example a petrol station or pub.

CHOOSING THE DAY FOR COMPLETION

It is important to agree the date of handover before exchange of contracts because the date has to be included in most agreements. If the precise date is not known for some reason then an end target date can be inserted, for example 'completion to take place within 3 months'. Where a franchise or similar business changes hands the final date for completion may be decided by the franchisor or controlling organisation; this is because the handover date may be dictated by training schedules, work cycles or other factors peculiar to the parent organisation. In these situations you may have little room to influence the timing.

The day selected for the handover could be your half day closing or the quietest trading day of the week or at the weekend. It may be easier to complete at the end of a month or at the end of a VAT period or at the end of the business financial year.

If all parties decide for their own reasons to make the change on a Sunday then an element of trust between you and your purchaser is needed. The legal completion would have to be done on the Friday or the Monday whilst the keys of the property would be passed over on the Saturday or Sunday after the stock valuation when your purchaser takes possession.

The other considerations which may militate against a weekend handover are the extra costs for weekend removal services, where used, and the fact that special arrangements may be needed for the electricity, gas, telephone and water meters to be read. On the other hand you may be able to call on more help from friends and relatives.

Normally you will propose the date for handover because you are best placed to judge the most convenient day from the business viewpoint. At the very least you should close while the stock is being valued although some stock valuers are capable of working whilst the business remains open for trade. Most business owners do decide to close for the day as there is so much to get through.

Most difficulties are ironed out in an amicable way and the practical task of the handover in the end goes quite smoothly.

SUMMARY

The detailed legal and technical work of solicitors and accountants involved in the transfer of the ownership of a business has not been described, as beyond the scope of this book. Instead this chapter has concentrated on the practical tasks required from you in readiness for the period between exchange and completion. The anxieties arising have been considered and suggestions made to lessen the burden. The various processes needed to transfer the ownership of different businesses have been explained. The differing ways of valuing the stock on handover have been outlined and finally some factors which affect your choice of date for handover are outlined.

In the next chapter we will consider the actions which take place between the exchange of contracts and completion.

CASE STUDIES

Chris's negotiation reaches a climax

Two days later the agent phones with another offer from the prospective purchaser. The new offer is half way between Chris's price and the original offer. The agent says that the purchaser will rent out his own property which is free of any mortgage and he has about 60% of the offer price in cash. The agent's opinion is that there should not be any difficulty in raising the balance. Chris refuses this offer, although he appreciates that the purchaser is unlikely to be able to increase it by very much. He acknowledges that he will be a good buyer.

The next day Chris telephones the agent to say that if the buyer can pay an extra £2,000 he will include the gas cooker, light fittings, curtains and microwave and he will pay the landlord's legal fees.

The deal is struck and all parties agree that before asking the solicitors to proceed the purchaser will meet his bank manager to obtain an offer of a loan in principle. Chris promises not to accept another offer provided the purchaser has received the offer of the loan and solicitors are instructed within four weeks.

Their son Matthew is delighted because he hates the smell of hot fat which pervades the house, but their daughter Elizabeth becomes sulky as she thinks that once again they are moving and she will miss her local friends.

Mabel finally makes up her mind

Mabel phones her solicitor and tells him the new price. He reminds her that he has not yet received the list of fixtures and fittings and asks her kindly where she is going to live. Mabel says she supposes that for a while she will live with her sister, and keep a look out for a nice little bungalow. The solicitor says that he knows of just the property where the owner has died. Mabel is not too keen and says she will think about it.

The purchaser phones one evening to say that they are now being pressed to move out: can they take over in four weeks' time? Their solicitor has said this is possible. Mabel is a bit panic stricken and vaguely remembers hearing that the process of handing over a post office can take three months (which on enquiry the Post Office confirms). She relays this to the purchaser who is annoyed because he thought his solicitor should have known. An alternative is worked out: after the handover Mabel will come in daily to run the post office until such time as it too is handed over.

Mabel suggests that they use her regular firm of stocktakers for the handover and share the cost. This is agreed.

How things turn out for Brian and Jill

Brian and Jill rush round to see the other property in the village. Their daughter Sue says she loves it. The house and property seem to suit their needs admirably and when told the price they realise that now they will have to bargain as purchasers. A price is negotiated but the vendors cannot move for six weeks. After two days haggling they agree on condition that Brian can move his building materials into the barn. On advice from his solicitor Brian is forced to concede that his stock of building materials can be moved onto the new property only after the exchange of contracts.

Local solicitors are appointed and manage to draw up the contract within ten days. When Brian visits the solicitor to sign, the solicitor points out that under the terms of the contract for sale they are not permitted to run a cattery within ten miles for two years. Brian is furious and threatens to storm out. He thinks the cattery would be a nice little earner where payments are made in cash and would be something to keep Jill out of his hair. Jill is secretly relieved as she was not looking forward to establishing and looking after a cattery whilst having a baby.

POINTS FOR DISCUSSION

1. How would you feel if you were one of the characters caught up in our business situations?

2. What questions do you want to put to your accountant, solicitor and agent?

3. How and when would you tell your own customers and suppliers about the change of ownership?

How to Write a Report

John Bowden

Written by an experienced manager and staff trainer, this well-presented handbook provides a very clear step-by-step framework for every individual, whether dealing with professional advisers, banks, customers, clients, suppliers or junior or senior staff. Contents: Preparation and planning. Collecting and handling information. Writing the report. Improving your thinking. Improving presentation. Achieving a good writing style. Making effective use of English. Illustrations. Choosing paper, covers and binding. Appendices, glossary, index.

John Bowden BSc (Econ) MSc has long experience both as a professional manager in industry, and as a Senior Lecturer running courses in accountancy, auditing, and effective communication, up to senior management level.

£7.99, 160pp illus. 1 85703 091 5. 2nd edition.
Please add postage & packing (UK £1 per copy.
Europe £2 per copy. World £3 per copy airmail).

How To Books Ltd, Plymbridge House, Estover Road,
Plymouth PL6 7PZ, United Kingdom.
Tel: (01752) 695745. Fax: (07152) 695699. Telex: 45635.

Credit card orders may be faxed or phoned.

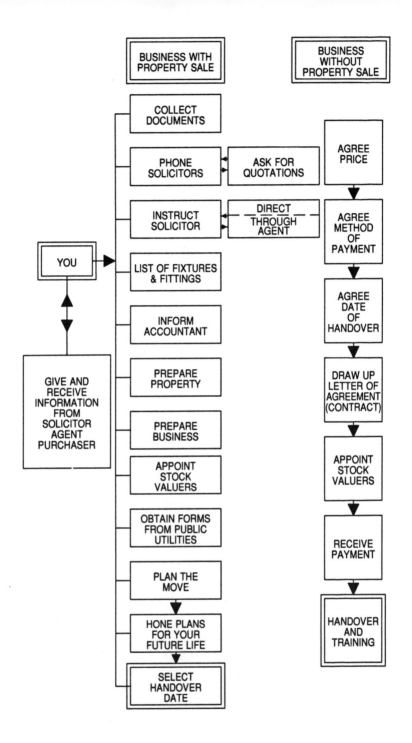

Fig. 34. Actions leading to exchange of contracts.

7
From Exchange to Completion

WHAT THIS CHAPTER WILL TELL YOU

At last the exchange of contracts has taken place and you can relax, feel the strain of selling is over. Now there remain only those practical arrangements before the big day of the handover.

Solicitors usually ask for four weeks between exchange of contracts and completion in which to finalise their own paperwork. Their work can be done in much less time, and with modern communication methods a few days can suffice. However you and your purchaser may need the four weeks to make all the arrangements, especially when living accommodation is involved.

CONTINUING TO TRADE

Of prime importance is the continuance of the business because the contract places such an obligation on you. You may well see more of your purchaser, particularly if he is a local person, and he may become a bit of a nuisance. He may ask to work with you for a week or two before completion. A training period may have been written into the contract. Provided there is a helpful attitude on both sides a period of working together can be a help, unless your feelings of helpfulness have already been exhausted. In this case controlling yourself can be a severe test for you both.

During the period between exchange and completion you can change the trading pattern to meet the wishes of your purchaser. For example your purchaser may have asked for a reduction in the stock level, or he may not want to take over certain lines or classes of goods. You can then cease to order certain goods and perhaps organise a special sale to dispose of unwanted items. Your purchaser may have decided not to take over some pieces of equipment, and so you will need to arrange for their removal or sale. There may be undertakings in the contract for certain building repairs to be completed before handover; you will need to ensure they are finished on time.

Most often, however, purchasers wish a business to continue to be run efficiently by the vendor without too much alteration and most vendors are content to comply. Your purchaser will probably wish to initiate any major changes himself after taking over the business rather than have these changes carried out by someone with no ongoing interest. Therefore your purchaser will probably stipulate in the contract that you refrain from making any major changes to the business or trading pattern during the period between exchange and completion.

Making final arrangements

There are actions which have to be put in hand immediately you have been told that the contracts have been exchanged. The following are not set out in a particular order, although some are dependent upon each other. This is not an exhaustive list, as some businesses have extra needs.

Settling dates
Fine tune the plan for the handover, agreeing dates and timing with your purchaser.

Informing the public utilities
Tell the public utilities the date of the handover so they can arrange to read gas, water and electricity meters, switch off telephone lines and so on.

Communicating with your solicitor
Check with your solicitor that he is taking all the essential actions with your bank, finance company and the separate licensing authorities to ensure that you comply with your obligations.

Arranging the insurance
Inform your insurers of the proposed change and date for completion. Although legally the ownership of the property and business will pass to your purchaser on exchange of contracts, he may not have arranged any or adequate insurance on the property, stock and the business. Should there be a disaster you may find yourself the loser. It is wiser to keep your insurance cover until completion rather than leave it to the purchaser who may be unaware of his responsibility.

Completing any building repairs
Put in hand any building repairs which have to be finished under the

terms of your contract for sale and any changes in the business agreed with your purchaser.

Communicating with your agent
Although he should have been informed by the solicitors, check that your agent is fully aware of the planned completion date. His invoice for his agency fee will be submitted to your solicitor who will include the figures in his final statement to you. Your solicitor will ask for your approval before payment.

Arranging for moving house
When living accommodation is involved in the sale you will need to confirm your booking with the furniture removers and arrange for the delivery of crates, boxes and packaging materials. Check on the help which friends and relatives have promised.

Confirming stock valuers booking
Confirm the date and starting time with details of any special terms agreed between you and your purchaser. The valuers will send you an information sheet showing what they need to ensure they can complete their task efficiently.

Checking with your accountants
Tell your accountant the handover date and check whether he needs any particular information or documents to complete your business accounts. This is particularly important when a limited company is being sold and share ownership being transferred.

Finalising the VAT deregistration
The local Customs and Excise must be told of the change of ownership and the intention to deregister or change the registration if another business is being bought or started. They will send you a form to complete. The VAT registration of a limited company remains with the company, but you still have to tell the Customs and Excise. The VAT charged on invoices for fees from solicitors and other professionals is normally reclaimable on your final VAT return. If you are unsure about the regulations and what is or what is not allowable, your local Customs and Excise office will advise.

Working with the franchisor
If the business is a franchise the franchisor will probably have the date of the handover already pencilled in. He will want this confirmed so that training arrangements can be booked and a new franchise

Final arrangements

Circle

Have you agreed all the operative dates and timings with your purchaser?	Yes/No
Have you told your staff about the change?	Yes/No
Have you told your customers?	Yes/No
Have you told your suppliers?	Yes/No
Have you agreed everything with your franchisor?	Yes/No
Have you told the public utilities?	Yes/No
Have you told your agent?	Yes/No
Have you confirmed with the stocktakers?	Yes/No
Have you checked with your accountant?	Yes/No
Have your bank and finance company been told?	Yes/No
Have you arranged property and building insurance?	Yes/No
Have you checked the licences with your solicitor?	Yes/No
Have you told the motor/tv licensing authorities?	Yes/No
Have you told the Customs and Excise?	Yes/No
Have you told all your relatives and friends?	Yes/No
Have you told all companies in which you hold shares?	Yes/No
Have you completed any building repairs?	Yes/No
Have you confirmed with the furniture removers?	Yes/No
Have you arranged for packing materials?	Yes/No
Have you arranged for extra help to move?	Yes/No
Have you thought of anything else to arrange?	Yes/No

Not all the above will apply for every business sale.

Fig. 35. Making final arrangements.

agreement issued to your purchaser. In the same way, if the business includes a sub post office then the local head post office will need confirmation.

Informing staff, customers and friends
There is no one way to tell the staff, but clearly it is better that staff are told by you rather than learn of it from customers, friends or suppliers.

Informing staff
You will have already discussed the question of taking over existing staff with your purchaser, and the staff will look to have their new contract of employment confirmed by the new owner. Staff anxiety can never be totally avoided and your aim should be to consider every way of lessening their worries by seeking the most considerate approach. New owners are usually happy to take over existing satisfactory and recommended staff.

Informing customers
Information to customers can take the form of a notice in the public area of the business, a handout, a mailshot, a press announcement or just word of mouth.

Informing suppliers and other creditors
Many suppliers on being told will immediately request information about your purchaser so that credit accounts can be opened with the least possible delay to avoid a break in the supply of goods. You could offer to pass on the names of his referees if you feel you want to be particularly helpful.

Suppliers and other creditors will also seek to present you with their final invoices and statements with any credits which may be applicable.

Notifying your change of address
Whilst trying to settle into and build up his new business your purchaser will not appreciate frequent and unnecessary telephone calls for you and your family or heaps of mail requiring readdressing. Mail can be readdressed by the post office or your purchaser but this does make for delays which could be annoying. The more change of address notices you send out to friends and relatives, the less hassle it will cause you and others.

Change of address information will be required by your bank, building society, motor vehicle licensing authority, TV licensing authority, premium bond office and so on plus any company or

```
┌─────────────────────────────────────────────────────────────┐
│                      New Management                          │
│                                                              │
│  Dear Customer,                                              │
│      For six years we have enjoyed your support and during   │
│  all that period we have endeavoured to give you the best    │
│  quality of service. As many of you know for the last few    │
│  months we have had some health problems which have          │
│  reluctantly brought us to a decision to sell the business.  │
│      Mr and Mrs Purchaser will be taking over on Monday      │
│  1st November and we are very confident that they will       │
│  continue to run the business efficiently. They have some    │
│  previous experience in this trade and we have talked        │
│  together about your needs at some length. We feel sure      │
│  that their ideas for improvements will benefit you. Please  │
│  give them your support.                                     │
│      You will understand that on 1st November the business   │
│  will be closed from 11am for the day for stocktaking. It    │
│  would help us all if newspapers can be collected whilst we  │
│  are open that morning and accounts paid up to and           │
│  including Sunday 31st October.                              │
│                                                              │
│  Yours sincerely,                                            │
│                                                              │
│                                                              │
│  John and Muriel Vendor                                      │
│                                                              │
└─────────────────────────────────────────────────────────────┘
```

Fig. 36. Sample handout notice to customers.

financial institution you may have dealings with or in which you and your family hold shares.

Preparing for the move

During the weeks before completion there will be a welter of activity as a result of the various announcements of the change in ownership. There will be forms to be filled in, notices to display in the business, letters to write, regular customers who will want to spend time talking about the change, interviews with the local press, staff worries to resolve and packing up of personal goods.

Business changeovers are much easier to manage when there is no accommodation involved but when you are moving house as well, you face all the arrangements over the new accommodation.

You may have felt the work of selling and at the same time buying a new home too daunting and have preferred not to think about the latter until your business is sold. You may have chosen to put your furniture in store and live in rented accommodation until finding a permanent home.

Dear Mr Wholesaler,

Re Account Number CT1234 – Vendors News, High Street .....

I am writing to inform you that I have sold my above business to Mr and Mrs Purchaser. The handover is planned for 1st November. I am arranging to send back all the accumulated items for credit with your next delivery on 27th October and any supplies to this business after that date should be invoiced to Mr and Mrs Purchaser at this address.

Can you please prepare my final statement as soon as possible so that I receive it before 1st November. After 5th November I shall be abroad for three months and therefore be unable to settle any outstanding accounts. Any correspondence can be sent to me care of the business and I shall collect it on my return.

If you wish to contact Mr and Mrs Purchaser prior to them taking over the business their address is ....
telephone number .....

Finally I should like to thank you and your staff for your pleasant co-operation over the last six years. Your representatives have been particularly helpful.

Yours faithfully

John Vendor

Fig. 37. Sample letter to suppliers.

However well you plan there are always unexpected emergencies and time should be allowed for them. It can be very flattering when one of your regular customers brings in a large gift at the last moment when everything is packed and all arrangements have been made. Other wellwishers will telephone at the last moment for a long chat.

Controlling your feelings

By the time such friendly gestures are received you may be so weary that you have difficulty in being civil and showing your appreciation. You may even come to regard them as the last straw – especially if you are feeling glad to get shot of a business you may not have enjoyed.

You may have spent years pouring time, thought and effort into the business and want to feel that when it is handed over all outstanding items have been dealt with and the business is handed over in a clean, neat and tidy condition.

You do not want to feel ashamed and upset by the thought that you have handed over a mess after years of effort. You may very well experience quite confused feelings ranging from loss to relief tinged with anxiety of what the future will hold.

Getting through the last day

This really starts the evening before. By then all the planning has been done, all the packing and preparation completed, all the arrangements for handover in place. You might plan a relaxed evening with friends or a meal out in a favourite restaurant or pub. You might have an extra early night or go for broke and have a late night because it may be hard to sleep anyway. You might just take it all in your stride and settle for a tranquilliser. It is all much simpler if your living accommodation is unchanged.

Friends can be helpful by providing regular cups of tea (or beer) and preparing the food for the day, whether snacks or a hot meal.

An early start is essential so that the handover can be completed as soon as possible. Probably your purchaser will experience even greater anxiety than yourself because of taking on the business and feeling the need to grasp the reins quickly and well. He knows there is much to learn very quickly and the sooner the changeover is completed the better it will be.

However much has been done in advance there are always snippets of helpful information to impart. The working of the till(s) and alarm systems, the foibles of various machines and even the location of light switches and stop cocks have to be pointed out. Local delivery routes need to be driven round and the individual needs of customers explained. Some purchasers have a quicker grasp than others of what they are being told; you will have to be patient and take care in giving explanations and demonstrating machines.

When the handover is on the same day as completion your solicitor should telephone you to confirm receipt of the money from your purchaser. You can then hand over the keys knowing all is well.

Getting paid for your stock

As already explained, your stock is sold to your purchaser at valuation. There are several ways you can be paid, bearing in mind that the stock value may not be known until after the banks have closed for the day.

Professional stock valuers should be able to provide a certificate of the stock value for you, your purchaser and your accountants within minutes of completing the count. The valuers will also present their invoice for immediate payment.

When independent stock valuers are not used both you and your purchaser will need to keep an accurate record of the agreed value of the stock for your respective accountants.

You will have told your purchaser the approximate value of the stock, and he should have planned his finances accordingly.

- When the stock value is relatively small, cash can be used and your purchaser should have it to hand. These businesses may be a café, fish and chips or greengrocery.

- When a larger sum is involved the usual method is simply for your purchaser to give you a cheque as soon as the total stock value is known and agreed.

- Alternatively you may have asked that he has available a certified cheque or banker's draft to cover the bulk of the estimated value of the stock and you agree to accept an ordinary cheque for the balance. If the total stock value fails to reach the amount of the certified cheque, you can refund the difference in cash or by cheque.

- Another method is to have the finance to cover the estimated value held by the solicitors and passed between them when the stock value is known.

Coping with a higher than expected stock value

Should the value of the stock prove much higher than the estimate or than the purchaser's resources, he will be embarrassed and you will be furious. The problem may have come about partly because to encourage a sale you have consistently understated the stock value and unwittingly misled your purchaser. His financial planning may have been based on your estimates.

Should a difficulty arise it always seems to occur at the end of a long day when everyone is tired out.

Although your purchaser will be in breach of his contract you have to be practical. Penalties written into the contract may be difficult to apply if the valuation is not completed until 10pm on a Saturday evening and nobody can decide what to do.

Fortunately finance not available to purchase the stock is an infrequent problem, but when it does arise the situation can become tricky and outside help should be sought. The presence of a solicitor, accountant, business transfer agent or stock valuer may help to resolve the problem amicably. They can act as a calming influence and work out a solution to the satisfaction of all.

There are several possible solutions. All may have limited appeal but you do have a choice.

Delaying part of the payment

Your purchaser may offer delayed payment for the outstanding balance. By accepting this alternative you are giving an unsecured loan for which you may not have budgeted. If the amount is substantial you should have a formal agreement prepared by your solicitor with the loan secured against an asset. You may think a loan is an unacceptable risk; after all, if your purchaser is taking the business on so tight a budget it is possible he might fail and you will not be paid.

For a relatively small amount your purchaser may offer a post-dated cheque, and an assurance that the resources to cover the cheque will be available by the time the cheque becomes due for presentation. Again there are the usual attendant risks.

Removing selected stock

Another alternative is for you to remove some stock. You may be able to return it to the wholesalers for credit, offer it to other retailers with whom you have developed a working relationship, sell it yourself through another outlet, or take a market stall for a few weeks. Removing some stock may involve additional valuation costs.

Only when you are satisfied that payment for the business and the stock has been made, or you are satisfied with the payment arrangements, should you hand the keys over. If you have any doubts talk to your solicitor and follow his advice.

SUMMARY

In this chapter the tasks required to achieve a smooth handover of the business have been outlined. The key to getting everything done and arranged with the minimum of discomfort and last minute overwhelming problems is very careful and accurate planning. It is also worth taking a few minutes to review the events and difficulties which arose when you first bought the business and learning from that experience. Through such a review you may well be able to understand better how your and your purchaser's needs have come together and base your actions and attitudes on this previous experience.

The proven advice from those people who have moved several times and have bought and sold businesses is that at the end of the moving day when all the essentials have been completed the first priority is to make the beds and the second priority is go to sleep. Everything which can be left should be left to the next day.

CASE STUDIES

Chris and Joan

Chris suddenly realises that, having (as he thinks) sold the business, he has no idea what to do nor how he will continue to support his family. To his horror he discovers that he is no longer entitled to unemployment benefit (in the back of his mind he had been relying on this).

Quite casually Chris chances on a job advertisement a week old in the local paper and decides to apply. Within a week he is offered the job and is pressed to start immediately. It seems too good an opportunity to miss. Their buyer also confirms that he has received a promise of finance and so solicitors are instructed. Joan struggles on her own with the lunch time openings and Chris helps out when he returns from work in the evening. Elizabeth continues to sulk, although she is cheered at the thought of not moving away; Matthew does what he can to help.

One evening the motor on the chipper burns out and Chris is faced with an unexpected large expense. He thinks about claiming on his insurance but he soon realises that he cancelled it as soon as contracts were exchanged. He talks with his purchaser who has not completed his proposal form and his solicitor tells him that a working chipper is listed in the contract and so Chris is obliged to buy one quickly. This upsets his tight budget. Rather than continue with the purchase of a house he feels he has no alternative to moving to rented accommodation.

Mabel

Mabel realises that time is slipping past and if she is not careful she will have to move before she is ready. She hardly noticed exchange taking place but does remember to ask her sister if she can use her spare room until she decides what to do. Her solicitor becomes very concerned and urges her to look at the little bungalow. He assures her it is nice and that she can rent it until she decides either to buy or to move elsewhere. She goes to see it on her half day and decides it will do – but she still wants her own furniture with her. Her sister is very relieved because much as she loves Mabel she was fearful of having her to live in.

As a moving gift, Mabel's sister and other members of the family decide to pay for a removal firm to do all the packing, removal and unpacking. Mabel and her sister are very sad at the thought of the destruction of the family home and can hardly bear to start throwing away the accumulation of a lifetime.

Brian and Jill

At the last moment before exchange Brian and Jill's purchasers find that due to a fall in the stock market the amount of money available is below the agreed price. They ask Brian to reduce his selling price so that they can go ahead. Brian refuses; why should he finance another's poor investment?

After three days the purchasers decide to raise a loan to cover the difference and tell Brian that the loan will be granted in two days. They ask if they can move their caravan to the kennels and live there in the interim. Without consulting his solicitor Brian agrees and he asks the solicitor to exchange on their purchase without waiting for the sale. The solicitor refuses and Brian threatens him with incompetence, stone walling and slowness. Patiently the solicitor explains that he cannot exchange on a purchase unless he is satisfied that the money will be available on completion day. Right now he is not satisfied, because Brian's contracts for sale have not been exchanged.

The purchasers bring their caravan but do not move in. Instead they live with relatives.

Three weeks later a critical survey from a building society puts further pressure on Brian to reduce the price. Brian is relieved that the purchasers are not living in their caravan at the kennels and with difficulty restrains himself from taking an axe to it. He refuses to budge on the price and after a further delay contracts are exchanged for completion a week later. The timing worked out well for Brian's purchase and he hired some casual labour to move the building materials. Jill is very quiet during all this and is making an effort to keep the kennels going and bring the account books up to date. She is feeling unwell and her daughter Sue is still being difficult.

POINTS FOR DISCUSSION

1. Our characters in the businesses fail to help themselves properly. What could you learn from them when you come to sell your own business?

2. In most business sales, problems arise which have to be overcome. What steps would you take to ensure that your move from the business can take place with the least disruption?

3. What will you miss most about your business and how are you going to feel about it?

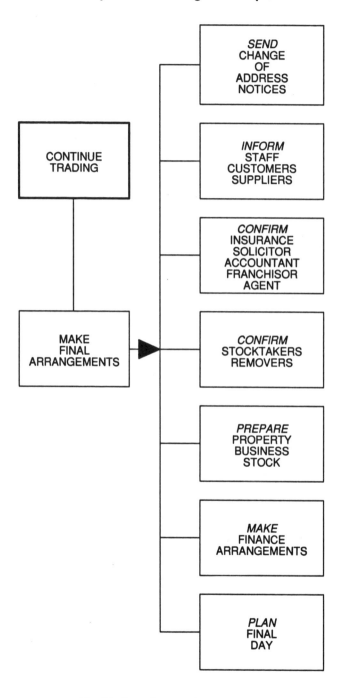

Fig. 38. Steps from exchange to completion.

8
Dealing with the Aftermath

You may suffer from a feeling of anti-climax after completion. You may feel a great relief. You may wonder if after all, you did the right thing? You may just feel very tired and have very little reaction.

You have exerted a great deal of effort to reach your goal of selling and now another effort is required to settle into a new way of life. However, a few items must still be tidied up before the business can finally be put behind you.

CLEARING UP YOUR FINANCES

Receiving and distributing the proceeds
If another business or property is being purchased simultaneously then the finance for this will have been despatched at once.

Your solicitor will have paid off any mortgages or loans you had with banks and building societies, and deducted conveyancing fees and other charges. He will have settled your agent's fees, and transferred the balance to you in accordance with any instructions you gave him in advance.

Your solicitor will have disbursed the funds as quickly as possible and you should receive a full **completion statement** within a week or two with receipted invoices. Some solicitors provide an interim statement almost immediately after the sale, with a final statement plus invoices following a few weeks later.

Preparing the final accounts
You should send all such documents to your accountant so that a final trading account and balance sheet can be prepared for submission to the Inland Revenue.

If the sale is of a limited company you may not receive all the money due until after a balance sheet has been prepared stating the company's financial position at the moment of sale. An interim payment will have been made, with the final payment deferred until all the figures have been agreed. When a limited company is involved it is therefore in your interest to gather all the relevant documents together as fast as possible and pass them to your accountant.

Settling outstanding trade accounts
It will take a few days before the final invoices relating to the business are received and payments made to your suppliers.

Payments receivable
In some businesses there will be payments to receive as well as to make. These could be against goods you have returned to suppliers, goods supplied to customers, commissions earned and so on. If a request for a fast settlement is explained tactfully then hopefully your invoice will be given some priority.

Payments due to suppliers
Similarly you should pay any outstanding invoices and statements as soon as you can so that all cheques can clear through the banks without delay.

Accounting documents
Your accountant will need all your normal documents including bank statements, invoices, cheque stubs, paying-in books, day books and so on which are associated with your end-of-year accounts. He will also want the invoices relating to the expenses for selling and moving. He will need confirmation (possibly from your solicitors) of the breakdown of the selling price into freehold property (or leasehold interest where appropriate), goodwill and fixtures, fittings and equipment. Anything else the accountant will ask for in the usual way.

Retaining accounting records
Whether yours was a limited company or not it will be a relief when all the paperwork has been finalised and all the old books of account, invoices, bank statements and so on quietly stored in an attic or back room cupboard. Although they will probably never be referred to again the accounts and all the supporting documentation should be kept for at least seven years so that if the business figures should be challenged by the Inland Revenue or other statutory body the original invoices, bank statements and other supporting documents can be produced.

Completing the final chores

You may find it a drag fulfilling your commitment to train your purchaser and wonder afterwards why you ever made such a promise. However in order to feel that you have completed the job well this still should be done with whatever enthusiasm you can muster.

Tidying up the last odds and ends will be an irritant when all you want to do is to enter the next stage of your life. However the longer you delay the harder these tasks will be to do.

PUTTING THE BUSINESS BEHIND YOU

Some purchasers can be over confident, make mistakes and then much later try to blame you for selling a business which is now less profitable than the genuine figures which you provided. You can find such an attack very hurtful after all the thought and effort you have made to build up the trade and the care which you took to sell your business as an efficient concern. Although you did your level best to train him and fulfil your obligations under the terms of your agreement, you may still be blamed for another's failure. You can comfort yourself with the knowledge you did everything you could. Unwittingly you may become the focus of your purchaser's inadequacy and you are helpless to do anything about it.

It is also common for businesses to take a dip in activity for a short period when they change hands. You may remind your purchaser that you had told him this was likely to happen and so draw the sting out of any disillusionment. As long as you have been straightforward and correct in the information supplied your purchaser can have no grounds to threaten you with litigation. However if you have misled him or have provided false information on which he has based his choice, you can be in considerable difficulty. 'Let the buyer beware' is at best only a thin defence in these circumstances.

Restrictions on your future activity

Within the terms of the contract for sale there will be a clause restricting you from setting up in competition to the business for a period, usually two years, within a geographical area. The geographical limit specified will vary according to the nature of the business and the spread of the business catchment. For example a newsagent in an urban area may have a total catchment spread over two miles from the shop; a saddler on the other hand may attract customers from a radius of twenty miles.

You will also be required to refer any enquiries for the goods and services provided by the business to the new owner – not to competitors. This is because you have sold and received payment for the goodwill of the business and therefore may not retain it by setting up in direct competition or deliberately damage it by referring business elsewhere. If you wish to continue to practise your skills, then you will need to ensure that you are not in contravention of any undertaking you have given your purchaser.

Looking at your feelings and the future

A sale can be like a diplomatic battle, the purchaser being the aggressor and you the defender. The purchaser makes the offers and you defend your position. The purchaser wants what you own on his terms; you defend your best interests to achieve an acceptable return.

Sometimes circumstances will favour you and at other times the purchaser. You have to be very aware of your strong points and your weak spots throughout the sale process. In some aspects you have to be very conciliatory and in others you can take a much stronger line. Decide in advance where the limits are for you, and try to assess where they lie for your purchaser.

There are many occasions during a sale where your limit may be tested by your purchaser. You need to be shrewd enough to know when to bend a little and when to remain firm so that your purchaser has to retreat or retire completely.

Inevitably mistakes are made, prices for businesses can be seen to rise and to fall after a sale has been achieved or an offer refused. You are usually in the weaker bargaining position because at the end of the day you may have to sell or close down. For your purchaser, even if he does not realise it, there is always the possibility of another business to buy or set up.

A legacy of bitter feelings towards your purchaser in your heart can be hard to live with and may last a long time. The sale of something as important as your business in which you have invested so much can prove more traumatic than you realise. Your business has represented your successes and failures, your good decisions and bad. It has preoccupied your thoughts over a number of years and for some it is the culmination of their working lives. It is not over dramatic to say that a well handled sale can make a great deal of difference to a person's attitudes, happiness and wellbeing for the rest of their life, whereas a badly handled sale can sour a person for evermore.

SUMMARY

In this book the process of selling a business has been traced and the actions and pitfalls have been outlined. The aim has been to provide a practical and useful guide to the whole process.

CASE STUDIES

Chris and Joan

Chris has another bright idea. Since his purchaser is going to rent out his house Chris asks him if he could become a temporary tenant until he decides whether to continue renting or to try to again buy a home. Although the house is inconvenient and small for their needs they all agree to the plan. The move goes smoothly, although delayed by the late arrival of the person to read the electricity meter, and there was a problem with the fish and the fish tank.

Chris looks forward to developing in his new job which he is enjoying, whereas Joan for a while feels uncomfortable in a temporary home. She is not sure how long they are staying and is constantly unsure what to unpack and what to leave packed. She spends a good deal of time just looking for things she thinks she needs. Matthew, although he disliked the fish and chip shop, has little to do and begins to think it was not so bad after all. Elizabeth is happy not to lose her friends and revels in being free of requests to help in the business.

Mabel

Mabel decides that on reflection she will buy the little bungalow rather than look around for another property. Her solicitor arranges for her to rent it until the conveyance can be put through.

Mabel's customers secretly plan to hold a party for her. They book the village hall for the evening before the move and only tell her that day while she is frantically trying to tidy up. Although Mabel is very touched she is dismayed because her party clothes have already been packed and she wants to look her best and does not want to disturb what has been done. She compromises and the party is a success, and everybody is most sympathetic – when for no obvious cause Mabel suddenly starts to weep in the middle of the evening. She confesses to her sister that she does not know how she is going to cope continuing to work in the post office for four weeks while major changes are being made to her old home and the shop.

The changeover goes smoothly. The stocktaker (who is also her business transfer agent) arrives on time and works steadily with little disturbance of the stock. Mabel is very hurt when she overhears the purchaser saying to the stocktaker that her lovely old polished wood serving counter is going to be thrown out and replaced by a secondhand aluminium glazed servover unit.

Several months later Mabel had a severe heart attack and died after two days in hospital.

Brian and Jill

Brian decides to use his own vehicle and men to make the move. Although Jill has asked for some clean boxes to pack their clothes Brian tells her not to worry he has it all in hand. Jill is concerned but the more she talks about it the more Brian reassures her that he has everything under control. Brian thinks Jill is fussing because she is pregnant and is sure that on the day their goods can be thrown into his vans. He cannot see the need for packing when they are only moving a short distance. The more Jill asks, the more he is sure that he is right and does nothing to acquire any boxes or packing material.

On the day of the move Jill has had enough and storms out with Sue leaving Brian with the chaos. The purchasers arrive early at half past nine expecting to move in and find little has been done in the house. Brian is at a loss as to how to cope with the household goods and so the purchasers set about organising them with the help of Brian's men.

Somehow the move of all their possessions is accomplished and Brian phones Jill at her mother's house to tell her. She is very upset about her behaviour and she feels that the move and having another child have in reality done little to solve their problems.

POINTS FOR DISCUSSION

1. Allowing for their personalities in what ways could each of our characters have sidestepped some of their difficulties?

2. Every move or business sale unleashes consequences. What do you foresee for yours?

3. What are you doing to mitigate the unwelcome consequences?

4. Have you set down the goals and dreams which you seek from your next business, property, job or retirement?

5. In what ways are you preparing for your future after the sale of your business?

The aftermath

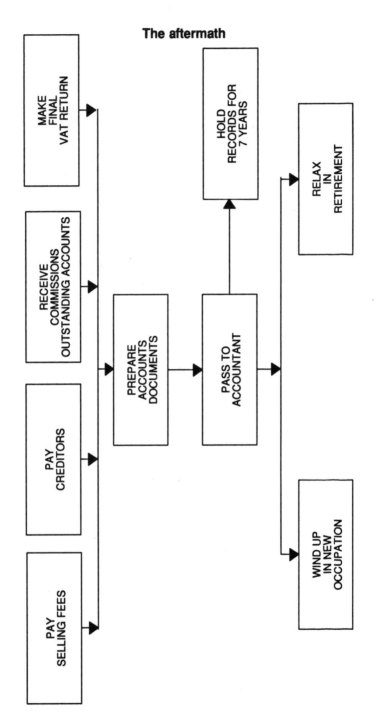

Fig. 39. The aftermath.

Glossary

Many of the definitions given in the glossary have been simplified for ease of explanation and understanding in relation to the content of this book. For a fuller interpretation which is technically accurate in your particular circumstances you need the advice of a solicitor or accountant.

Advertisers pack

An information pack produced by publishers setting out all potential advertisers need to know to place an advertisement in their publication. Sometimes called a media pack.

Back copy

An out of date issue of a magazine, newspaper or journal which may be used as an example of the publication.

Balance sheet

A statement of the financial assets and debts of a business at a given date.

Bankruptcy

The state of being no longer able to fulfil your financial obligations. See also **insolvent**.

Bookkeeping

Maintaining written records of all the financial transactions of a business.

Business plan

Normally refers to an annual plan or chart detailing the anticipated financial movements month by month for a business. Some plans lay out the future development objectives of the business.

Business transfer agent

A person or firm who acts as an agent to seek a purchaser for a business and negotiate a sale. Sometimes appointed by prospective purchasers to find a business.

Capital gains tax (CGT)
A tax based on the gain accruing to assets and businesses when disposed of. Individuals' principal private residences are excluded from the tax liability.

Chartered surveyor
A qualified member of a professional body specialising in surveying and valuing property.

Classified advertisements
The grouping of small advertisements under broad headings such as 'Businesses for Sale'. (see **lineage and display advertisements**).

Completion
The moment when the business and/or property is handed over in exchange for the balance of the agreed purchase price.

Contract of sale
A formal agreement to sell a property and/or business on a certain date, usually drawn up by solicitors.

Damages
Financial compensation awarded by a court of law (eg for breach of contract).

Display advertisement
An advertisement in which a block of space is booked and filled with an individually designed advertisement.

District valuer
An independent property valuer appointed by a District Council to assess and value domestic and business properties.

Estate agent
An agent who promotes the sale of freehold and leasehold property, usually domestic, and advises on values.

Exchange of contracts
The moment when a planned sale becomes binding on both parties, with the handing over of a deposit.

Financial institution
An organisation whose prime activity is banking, deposit-taking, investment, insurance, pensions, and making loans to individuals and businesses.

Forced sale value
A market value which is bound to achieve a sale quickly.

Franchise agreement
The formal document between two parties recognising the granting of a franchise by a franchisor to a franchisee and detailing the terms and geographical area.

Franchisee
A person or business holding a franchise.

Franchisor

A person or business who issues to another the rights to a service or process, normally for a geographical area, in return for payment.

Freehold

A property owned permanently with or without a mortgage, and with full rights of usage subject to any covenants and Local Authority permissions.

Full repairing lease

A lease in which the onus for all the inside and outside decoration, maintenance and repairs to the property is the full responsibility of the lessee.

Goodwill

The value of the privilege and reputation granted by the seller of a business to the purchaser, of trading as his recognised successor, with the benefit of ready formed connections with customers and suppliers.

Gross profit (annual)

The difference in a year between the purchases and the sales (allowing for changes in the value of the stock). (See also **net profit**).

House style

The printing, layout, spelling and abbreviation conventions adopted by a publisher.

Insolvent

Being unable to pay debts as they fall due for payment.

Intellectual property

Intangible rights which are owned, for example a patent, a copyright.

Internal repairing lease

A lease in which only the internal decoration and maintenance are the responsibility of the **lessee**. Sometimes shop fronts are included. The lessor remains responsible for external and roof maintenance.

Lease

A contract between two parties by which one grants to another land and/or premises for a term of years in return for rent.

Lessee

A person who has contracted to receive the use of land or property for a term of years and for which he has undertaken to pay rent.

Leasehold

The holding of property under the terms of a **lease**, permitting the **lessee** the right to carry out a specified activity.

Lessor
A **freehold** owner of land or property who has made or is offering a grant of his land or property for a term of years to another in return for rent.

Licence agreement
Similar to a **franchise agreement**.

Licence to assign
The formal permission given by a landlord **(lessor)** to his **lessee** that the lease may be passed to the new proposed lessee. Usually drawn up by the landlord's solicitor.

Licensee
Similar to a **franchisee**.

Licensor
Similar to a **franchisor**.

Limited company
A legal trading entity, owned by shareholders and managed by directors. It is responsible for its debts up to the limit of its share capital. Legislation closely defines what a limited company may do, and how it may do it.

Lineage
Straightforward word advertisements in the columns of newspapers, magazines and journals, charged by the line. Usually **classified**.

Lock-up
Business premises or other property not having any living accommodation.

Market value
The estimated sum which will attract purchasers to view and achieve a sale in a reasonable time.

Mixed agency agreement
An agreement which permits a business owner to appoint more than one agent to act for him whilst remaining responsible for a fee only to the agent who introduces the successful purchaser.

Mortgage
A loan secured against a property. If the loan is not repaid, the lender can demand that the property be sold to repay the debt.

Net profit (annual)
The gross profit less the running expenses of the business (see also **gross profit**).

Newsagent
A regular dealer in newspapers and periodicals.

Profit and loss account
This account is sometimes known as 'The Trading and Profit and Loss Account'. It summarises income and expenditure over a

stated period (eg one year).

Rate card

A card or brochure produced by magazine and periodical advertising departments detailing their advertising rates and conditions.

Rateable value

A notional 'annual value' placed on the business by the District Valuer, intended to represent a fair annual rent in 1990.

Retirement Sale

A sale of a business prompted by the owner planning to retire. Any profit on such a disposal may qualify for tax relief called retirement relief.

Schedule of dilapidations

List of building repairs which are the responsibility of the lessee.

Semi display advertisements

Lineage advertisements separated by a mark, box or line from other advertisements in their column.

Small business

Sole proprietor or family run concern possibly employing a few full or part time staff, or a small independent branch of a larger concern.

Sole agency agreement

In return for a reduced fee the owner agrees to appoint one agent whilst still remaining free to seek a purchaser himself. The fee becomes payable only if the agent introduces the purchaser.

Sole agency with sole selling rights

This agreement binds the owner so that however the purchaser is introduced the owner pays a fee to the agent. The fee is usually at a lower rate.

Stock valuer

Similar to **stocktaker**.

Stocktaker

A person or company undertaking the valuing and/or listing of the stock of a business.

Subject to contract

An offer or agreement which is not to be made binding on either party until formal contracts for sale have been drawn up and approved.

Trading accounts

The accounts which show the total sales and costs of a business over a period of time, usually one year.

Transitional relief (on rates)

A system of reduced **uniform business rate** to take into account inequalities when the change in the business rating system was introduced.

True net income

The income achieved from a business after allowing for only those costs directly attributable to the running of the business.

Uniform business rate

A poundage rate on the **rateable value** which is set nationally each year for all business premises.

Warranty

A specific and legally binding promise in a written contract.

Useful Addresses

TRADE PERIODICALS

Telephone numbers include the revised codes effective from August 1994.

Asian Business
8/16 Coronet Street
London N1 6HD
Tel: (0171) 729 5453

Asian Trader
1 Silex Street
London SE1 0DW
Tel: (0171) 928 1234

Bakers Review
171 High Street
Rickmansworth
Herts WD3 1SN
Tel: (01923) 777000

The Bookseller
12 Dyott Street
London WC1A 1DF
Tel: (0171) 836 8911

British Baker
Maclaren House
19 Scarsbrook Road
Croydon
Surrey CR9 1QH
Tel: (0181) 688 7788

CTN/Confectioner/Tobacconist/Newsagent
Maclaren House
19 Scarsbrook Road
Croydon
Surrey CR9 1QH
Tel: (0181) 688 7788

Cabinet Maker & Retail Furnisher
Benn Publications
Sovereign Way
Tonbridge
Kent TN9 1RW
Tel: (01732) 364422

Caterer & Hotel Keeper
Quadrant House
The Quadrant
Sutton
Surrey SM2 5AS
Tel: (0181) 652 3737

Convenience Store
Broadfield Park
Crawley
Sussex RH11 9RT
Tel: (01293) 613400

DIY Trade Buyers Guide
Benn Publications
Sovereign Way
Tonbridge
Kent
TN9 1RW
Tel: (01732) 364422

DIY Week
Benn Publications
Sovereign Way
Tonbridge
Kent
TN9 1RW
Tel: (01732) 364422

Daltons Weekly
W. I. Tower
St George's Square
New Malden
Surrey KT3 4JA
Tel: (0181) 949 6199

Dog World
9 Tufton Street
Ashford
Kent TN23 1QN
Tel: (01233) 621877

Drapers Record
Maclaren House
19 Scarsbrook Road
Croydon
Surrey CR9 1QH
Tel: (0181) 688 7788

Electrical & Radio Trading
Quadrant House
The Quadrant
Sutton
Surrey SM2 5AS
Tel: (0181) 652 3024

Estates Gazette
151 Wardour Street
London W1V 4BN
Tel: (0171) 437 0141

Fish Friers Review
New Federation House
4 Greenwood Mount
Leeds LS6 4LQ
Tel: (01532) 307009

The Grocer
Broadfield Park
Crawley
Sussex RH11 9RT
Tel: (01293) 613400

Grower
50 Doughty Street
London WC1N 2BR
Tel: (0171) 405 8388

*Hairdressers Journal
International*
Quadrant House
The Quadrant
Sutton
Surrey SM2 5AS
Tel: (0181) 652 3737

Hardware & Garden Review
111 St James Road
Croydon
Surrey CR9 2TH
Tel: (0181) 684 9659

Horse & Hound
Room 2101
Kings Reach Tower
Stamford Street
London SE1 9LS
Tel: (0171) 261 2161

Independent Grocer
Quadrant House
The Quadrant
Sutton
Surrey SM2 5AS
Tel: (0181) 652 8277

Lloyds List
Lloyds of London Press
Sheepen Place
Colchester
Essex CO3 3LP
Tel: (01206) 772277

Meat Trades Journal
Maclaren House
19 Scarsbrook Road
Croydon
Surrey CR9 1QH
Tel: (0181) 688 7788

Melody Maker
26th Floor
Kings Reach Tower
Stamford Street
London SE1 9LS
Tel: (0171) 261 5519

Morning Advertiser
Elvian House
Nixey Close
Slough
Berks SL1 1NQ
Tel: (01753) 810503

Off-Licence News
Broadfield Park
Crawley
Sussex RH11 9RT
Tel: (01293) 613400

Retail World
Greater London House
Hampstead Road
London NW1 7QQ
Tel: (0171) 388 3171

Scottish Grocer
Bergius House
20 Clifton Street
Glasgow G3 7LA
Tel: (0141) 331 1022

Shoe & Leather News
Maclaren House
19 Scarsbrook Road
Croydon
Surrey CR9 1QH
Tel: (0181) 688 7788

Sports Trader
146-7 Temple Chambers
Temple Ave
London EC4Y 0BP
Tel: (0171) 583 6463

Toy Trader
Turret House
171 High Street
Rickmansworth
Herts WD3 1SN
Tel: (01923) 777000

Travel Trades Gazette UK & Ireland
Morgan Grampion House
Calderwood Street
London SE18 6QH
Tel: (0181) 855 7777

PROFESSIONAL BODIES

Advertising Association
Abford House
15 Wilton Road
London SW1
Tel: (0171) 828 2771

Advertising Standards Authority
Brook House
Torrington Place
London WC1
Tel: (0171) 580 5555

Association of British Chambers of
Commerce
9 Tufton Street
London SW1P 3QB
Tel: (0171) 222 1555

Association of British Insurers
51 Gresham Street
London EC2V 7HQ
Tel: (0171) 600 3333

British Institute of Management
Management House
Cottingham Road
Corby
Northants NN1 1TT
Tel: (01536) 204222

British Insurance & Investment
Association
BIBA House
14 Bevis Marks
London EC3A 7NT
Tel: (0171) 623 9043

Chartered Association of Certified
Accountants
29 Lincoln's Inn Fields
London WC2
Tel: (0171) 242 6855

Incorporated Association of
Building Engineers
Jubilee House
Billingbrook Road
Northampton
NN3 8NW
Tel: (01604) 404121

Incorporated Society of Valuers
and Auctioneers
3 Cadogan Gate
London SW1X 0AS
Tel: (0171) 235 2282

Institute of Chartered Accountants
of England and Wales
PO Box 433
Chartered Accountants Hall
Moorgate Place
London EC2P 2BJ
Tel: (0171) 920 8100

Institute of Chartered Accountants
of Scotland
27 Queen Street,
Edinburgh EG2 1LA
Tel: (0131) 225 5673

Institute of Management
Consultants
32 Hatton Garden
London EC1N 8DL
Tel: (0171) 242 2140

Institute of Revenue Rating and
Valuation
41 Doughty Street
London WC1N 2LF
Tel: (0171) 831 3505

Institution of Business Agents
353 Warwick Road
Solihull
West Midlands
B91 1BQ
Tel: (0121) 708 1884

Law Society
113 Chancery Lane
London WC2
Tel: (0171) 242 1222

Royal Insitute of Chartered
Surveyors
12 Great George Street
London SW1P 3AD
Tel: (0171) 222 7000

Small Firms Information Service
Abell House
John Islip Street
London SW1P 4LN
Dial 100 and ask for
FREEPHONE ENTERPRISE

OTHER CONTACTS

Business rates	See the Phone Book under the local District or City Council.
Business transfer agents	See *Yellow Pages*, *Daltons Weekly*, local newspapers.
District valuer	See the Phone Book under 'Valuation officer'.
Environmental health officer	See the Phone Book under the local District or City Council.
Local authority	See the Phone Book under '..... City Council'. '..... District Council', '..... Town Council', '..... County Council'.
Office of Fair Trading	Office of Fair Trading, Field House, 15-25 Bream's Buildings, London EC4A 1PR. Tel: (0171) 269 8800.
Planning officer	See the Phone Book under the Local District or City Council.
Public library	See the Phone Book under 'Libraries'.
Stocktakers	See *Yellow Pages* under 'Stocktaking Services'.
Tax enquiries	See the Phone Book under 'Inland Revenue'.
VAT enquiries	See the Phone Book under 'Customs and Excise Department'.
Useful magazines & journals	Refer to *Brad*, *Directory of Publishing*, and *Small Press Year Book* available at central public libraries.

Further Reading

Estate Agency Act 1979 (HMSO).

How to Buy & Run a Shop, Iain Maitland (How To Books, 1992, 2nd edition).

How to Buy & Run a Small Hotel, Ken Parker (How To Books, 1992).

How to Do Your Own Advertising, Michael Bennie (Northcote House/ How To Books, 1990).

How to Sell a Business, Jason Cross (Kogan Page).

How to Write a Press Release, Peter Bartram (How To Books, 1993).

Property Misdescriptions Act 1991 (HMSO).

Realising the Value of a Business – A Buyer's and Seller's Guide, Barrie Pearson (Livingstone Fisher Associates PLC).

Index